MW00904401

SOMETHING BORROWED, SOMETHING TRUE

Ancient Civilization as Biblical Background

**by
Bob Mayfield**

Dear Mary Nell,
I hope you enjoy
my book!
Bob Mayfield

Copyright © 2014 **by Robert C. Mayfield (Bob Mayfield)**
All rights reserved.

ISBN: 1492238201
ISBN 13: 9781492238201
Library of Congress Control Number: 2013915875
CreateSpace Independent Publishing Platform
North Charleston, South Carolina

THIS BOOK IS DEDICATED TO ALL OF THE INTERESTED AND INTERESTING STUDENTS WHO ATTENDED MY CLASSES OVER THE YEARS. IT IS WRITTEN IN APPRECIATION OF THE QUESTIONS THEY RAISED AND IN RESPONSE TO THEIR REQUESTS FOR A SINGLE VOLUME INCORPORATING THESE IDEAS.

The cover illustration of Shamash, the Akkadian/Babylonian Sun God, was crafted by artists Hannah Barnes and Autumn Bussen. Ms. Barnes is Associate Professor of Painting at Ball State University. Ms. Bussen is a graduate student in art at Indiana University, Bloomington. With the exception of the map shown in Figure 1, they prepared all illustrations for this book.

"Most people, in fact, will not take the trouble to find out the truth, but are much more inclined to accept the first story they hear."

Thucydides, *The History of the Peloponnesian War*, 431 BCE.

"No subject of science seems to be more misunderstood by those who are not biologists than the doctrine of evolution... When one has been completely informed concerning evolution, he realizes that it does not contradict the Bible in any serious way, but really teaches the same fundamental truths from a different perspective."

John M. and Merle C. Coulter, Introduction to *Where Evolution and Religion Meet*, 1924. (John Coulter, President of Indiana University from 1891 to 1893, served as the head of the Department of Botany at the University of Chicago until 1928.)

"Good historians are always aware that history as well as life knows only developments, and that absolute origins escape them. There is always something earlier."

Jean Bottero, <u>Mesopotamia: Writing, Reasoning, and the Gods</u>, 1992.

My well-read sister, Doris Rutherford, had just finished Will and Ariel Durant's 11-volume master work, <u>The Story of Civilization</u>. Teasing, I asked her to summarize, in 25 words or less, what she had learned. She answered: *"That's easy! Women have been discriminated against forever."*

When I returned from Boston in 1984, there was a large sign in South Austin beside a fundamentalist church that also sponsored a K-12 school. The sign advertised the school, and was placed near the curb of a busy street. To establish the school's conservative credentials, those responsible had added a message near the bottom of the sign in large letters. The message: the Bible is infallible. The problem was—they misspelled infallible.

CONTENTS

FOREWORD

Anyone who writes about ancient civilization is deeply indebted to the archaeologists who first discovered, translated, and announced to the world their discoveries and research. My special debt is to Professor Samuel Kramer of the University of Pennsylvania, whose brilliant works first illuminated ancient Sumeria for me, and to Diana Wolkstein, who collaborated with him.

The works cited in this book were my primary sources, but there are many other volumes that are useful for those interested in pursuing similar themes. There is an introductory bibliography at the end of this book.

I began presenting this material to adult classes in the late 1970s. None of my many students, including retired ministers, historians, and anthropologists, were familiar with the ideas and events covered in those presentations. The well-educated seniors in SAGE at the University of Texas in Austin, in particular, have asked that I prepare a book from my lectures, and this is that book.

My own experiences and explorations have always been a part of what I presented, too. Loraine and I recently celebrated our 62nd wedding anniversary. During most of our married life, except for two year-long trips to India for research and my seven years in university administration at Boston University, I taught courses that dealt with both South Asia and East Asia.

My graduate work at the University of Washington, the research for the courses I taught, and the experience of living in India in 1957-58 and 1966-67 gave me an interest in the major religions of those areas centered on India and China. A common theme, most familiar to us as the Golden Rule, began to emerge in four of these faiths and philosophies—Confucianism, Buddhism, Taoism, and Jainism—about 2,500 years ago. However, it appears earliest in a statement by the Hindu sage, prophet, and scholar Vagnavalkya, writing in the seventh century before the Christian era:

"It is not our religion, still less the color of our skin, that produces virtue; virtue must be practiced. Therefore, let no one do to others what he would not have done to himself."

Although this theme is a version of the Golden Rule, it gives way to a negative stance. The founders of the four faiths—Confucius, Buddha, Lao Tzu of Taoism, and Mahavira of Jainism—are all credited with saying this in a variety of ways, but always with that negative formulation. In *Matthew 7:12*, Jesus would say it in a straightforward, positive way: *"Do unto others as you would have others do unto you."*

In 1976, we were living in Medfield, Massachusetts, and were members of a lively United Church of Christ congregation that met on Main Street in a white wooden building with a tall steeple. It was New England to the core. Members of our adult Sunday school class asked me to present a lesson on "the geography of the Holy Land." I tried to argue out of it on the grounds that I had never been there and had never studied that part of the world, but they persisted. I gave it a try.

It was easy enough to come to grips with the physical features of the region and, after a little reading, even with the complex geopolitical history of the area over the years. However, I soon realized that I didn't know much of anything about the origins of the ideas expressed in the Old Testament Bible.

After some off-and-on, spare-time reading of the many books related to that subject, I finally remembered something I had enjoyed reading many years earlier in an introductory course in sociology. The professor in that class had the good sense to include material from other disciplines. One short piece was from Ralph Linton's remarkable introduction to anthropology, _The Study of Man_, which was written in 1936, and will be as pertinent in 2036. Reading it again reminded me of the perspective required to make sense of what I was reading.

The selection is now popularly known as *"The 100% American."* By following one day in the life of an American man, Linton informs the reader that almost all of the basic material goods in our lives originated outside our country, outside our culture, and long before the present day. From our beds and bed covers, to our clothes, slippers, and shoes, to our food and our glass windows, to our umbrellas, to just about everything in our daily experience—all were derived from others prior to the founding of our nation.

Linton ended the piece with the following: *"—he reads the news of the day (printed in characters invented by ancient Semites on material invented in China by a process invented in Germany). As he absorbs the accounts of foreign troubles, he will (if he is a good conservative citizen) thank a Hebrew deity in an Indo-European language that he is 100% American."*

After reading that again, I realized that we are all *"100% Christians," "100% Jews,"* or whatever. Many of the sources for the Old Testament extend so far back in time that we no longer know their origins, because those were lost from common knowledge many centuries before they were recorded. Understandably, we take a great many of our religious teachings for granted.

Most likely, the early Hebrew writers of the Old Testament didn't know the origins of the stories they were recording.

Perhaps, given the subject matter of their oral traditions, and the great length of time that had passed since those were first introduced, the recorders simply asserted what others had claimed much earlier—a divine source.

It is also understandable that they would make a selective claim to these broad traditions on behalf of their own faith. And, to the extent that the overall outcome was to raise them (and us) to higher levels of spiritual understanding, then the assumption of a divine origin makes sense also. God seems to love evolution.

CHAPTER ONE
Partly Personal

This book is about the cultural evolution of ancient traditions which contributed to the Old Testament books of the Bible. There are substantial elements of such evolution in the development of all of the world's major religions and their sacred texts. Not all scriptures come to us through a revelation, a word, or stone tablets.

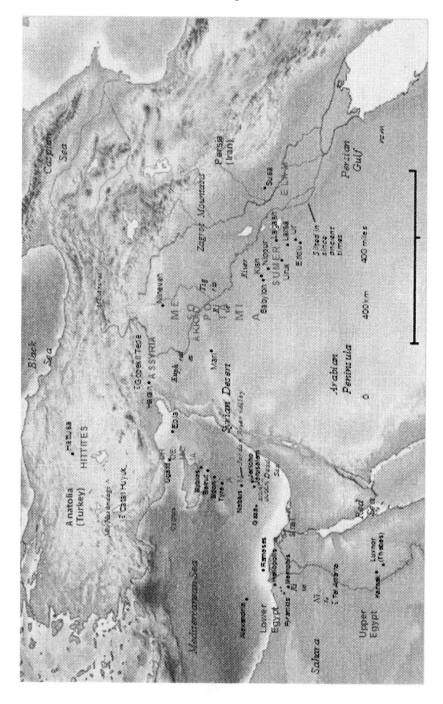

Figure 1: Sumeria, Canaan, and Egypt

Many of the concepts and stories found in the Old Testament can be traced back to their beginnings in Sumeria (Sumer), which was located in the southern third of Mesopotamia (modern-day Iraq). They may have originated much earlier in pre-Sumerian societies, but because the Sumerians developed the first written language, their hymns, stories, myths, and values were the first to be recorded. These were adopted far beyond Sumeria, extending into all of central and northern Mesopotamia and to Turkey, Syria, and Canaan; on the trade routes to Egypt and up on the Iranian plateau; and on the trade routes to Afghanistan and India.

These early Sumerian beliefs were used and transformed by the Akkadians, the Babylonian Amorites, the Assyrians, the Kassites, the neo-Babylonian Chaldeans, the Hittites, the Hurrians, and others who held sway in at least part of Mesopotamia before the arrival of the Persians, the Greeks and the Romans. Mesopotamian people built their mythology on a written Sumerian heritage which they never abandoned but modified as they saw fit.

One of the several biblical recorders who included the ancient mythological lore of non-Semitic people gave us a memorable anachronism when he noted that Abraham left "Ur of the Chaldeans." No, Abraham (Abram) left Ur of the *Sumerians* about 1500 years before any Chaldeans ever ruled that city. Abraham's father, Terah, named after a Mesopotamian moon god, decided that his family had to leave Ur. He took them to Haran in southeastern Turkey. The family settled in that crossroads city because it was their ancestral home.

Then, as *Genesis* reports, Abraham and parts of his extended family went on to Canaan, where drought eventually forced them to Egypt. Abraham and his family prospered until they were expelled by the pharaoh for quite good reasons. Abraham's knee-trembling suggestion to the border guards that Sarah was his sister, not his wife, led her to the pharaoh's bed and a debasement of the pharaoh's personal morality. The writers of the Old Testament enjoyed that story so much that they used variations of it three times in different places.[1]

The need for more than a decent meal brought about a second move to the Nile delta by Abraham's grandson, Jacob, and Jacob's family. It was safely made under the protection of Jacob's youngest son, Joseph. As you may remember, Joseph had been sold earlier by his brothers to traders on their way to Egypt, where he prospered and ascended to a position of authority. Unfortunately, Jacob's desperate move to Egypt to escape drought led to something worse—a long period of slavery for the Hebrew people.

According to *Exodus* 12:40, the Hebrews spent 430 years in Egypt, where their numbers increased rapidly, although most of their time there must have been spent in bondage. Joseph was a powerful non-Egyptian administrator in the employ of foreign conquerors called the Hyksos, who occupied northern Egypt and controlled southern Egypt through appointed pharaohs.

Read the entire story of Joseph in Exodus and you will quickly understand why his family's descendants were enslaved. Joseph's edicts destroyed not only the livelihood of the Egyptian people under Hyksos domination, but also their freedom, in successively harsher and deadlier steps. Once Hyksos rule was ended by an Egyptian rebellion, a new line of pharaohs came to power who would never admit to knowing Joseph.

With the Hebrew people's departure from Egypt around 1240 BCE and their resettlement in Canaan, they again found themselves in an area with a long history of predominantly Mesopotamian culture and a mix of Egyptian and locally-developed myths.

In writing the Old Testament, the Hebrew scribes often borrowed, transformed and retold that same mix of Mesopotamian and Egyptian ideas, stories and beliefs. But these elements were woven in with stories and beliefs that reflected their own more recent history as a people. Some of these were beginning to be written down about five centuries after their return to Canaan from the land along the Nile. Before that, they must certainly have been part of an oral tradition sustained by memory.

After a culturally disturbing captivity in Babylon from 587 to 538 BCE, the Jews wasted little time completing the recording of their scripture into the books that made up their Tanakh. (In a rearranged order, the Tanakh became what is known to Christians as the Old Testament.) It is quite understandable that the Jews would extract from their wide-ranging cultural experience what was most meaningful to them and make it theirs. In most instances of their selective borrowing, they were refining the ideas and improving the poetry, but as we will see, they made the writings more patriarchal as well.

Eventually, Canaan and the Jews would be conquered by the Greeks, whose culture was unacceptable to the Jews. Much to the Jews' discomfort, after the Greeks came the Romans, who borrowed and reinforced Greek culture with a very heavy hand.

———

Following the evolutionary trail of the Old Testament never evoked any faith concerns for me. In fact, knowing more about what actually happened and when removed much of my normal burden of doubt.

One of the most difficult tasks for anyone with an interest in the origins of the Old Testament is to develop an acceptable chronology from Ur to the Exodus. My efforts were no exception. Nothing seemed to work, whether I started from Abraham's departure from Ur and worked forward, or whether I started from the Exodus and worked back.

Then I remembered how the Sumerians had solved their own chronological problems in developing a list of kings, for example. Whenever those early writers had gaps they couldn't fill, they just extended the life spans of the historical figures whose names they knew to miraculous lengths. Biblical scribes also found that to be a convenient device in resolving their own chronological shortcomings.

To make a workable and believable chronology, I also had to make assumptions. For one, I assumed that the Abraham who went from Ur to Haran was not the quite elderly Abraham who led his extended family to Canaan, but was, more likely, a descendant given the same name. Naming a child after an important ancestor was commonplace. No bones belonging to a human of our species who lived anywhere near 175 years have ever been found, and we have *Homo sapiens sapiens* remains that date back 160,000 years.

Until the early 1990s, I had presented this material only to adult Sunday school classes. Then I began presenting a variety of six-day short courses for SAGE, one of several University of Texas programs for seniors who are interested in keeping their brains renewed. In the second year of teaching for SAGE, I gave a detailed seminar covering the Jews' cultural borrowing from Mesopotamia, Egypt, and Canaan, and from their Babylonian captivity. It was comparatively short in duration but reasonably high in impact, judging by the favorable student response. The seminar was called *"Ancient Civilization as Biblical Background,"* and I presented it eight times over the years, revising and updating it as I went along.

One could create a considerable library of readily available, interesting, but sometimes conflicting material on the cultural background of the Bible. Books by recognized scholars who have maintained a long-standing and compelling interest in the truth are by far the best sources, and that is so even when the authors don't entirely agree with each other's findings. There are a large and growing number of such books.

As you might expect, when one searches the Internet for topics related to religion, many of the sites that appear are biased with a particular doctrinal view. Far too many of the sites related to ancient civilization are filled with fanciful nonsense and sloppy fabrications promoting everything from New Age cults to fake jewelry to rock bands.

Money-driven sales pitches, which often appear first in search results, are numerous and tedious, but deeper scholarly articles are there also. A number of extremely useful online sites are dedicated solely to the literary achievements of the Sumerians.

Well-written books about science and religion, the relationship between the two, and the supposed conflicts between them, are also worth your time and effort, but you need to chart your own path through that maze of ideas.

For me, there is no conflict between the theory of evolution and my own understanding that we are still undergoing creation in both biological and cultural terms, and that includes our religion. As the Jesuit theologian and paleontologist, Teilhard de Chardin, liked to put it, we are still in the process of becoming.

He also noted, somewhat to the displeasure of the Vatican at the time: *"One may say that until the coming of Man it was natural selection that set the course of morphogenesis and cerebration, but that after Man it is the power of invention that begins to grasp the evolutionary reins."*[2] He died in 1955 before many of our dramatic advances in technology had begun to change the world.

Wondering about the true nature of the Creative Spirit at work in the Universe has come easily; finding satisfying answers has been harder. In this book, largely out of lifelong habit, I will often call that Creative Spirit "God." I do that with the understanding that many of our forebears have called it, quite appropriately, "Goddess," along with a great many other names.

———

One night around 4 a.m., I woke with the odd notion that there were several things at work that could have kept this Creative Spirit from experiencing boredom over the 13.8 billion years that have passed since the Big Bang.

First came the awesome process of forming, reforming and expanding the Universe in all its magnificent scope and diversity. Our access to the Hubble telescope has been a fairly recent delight, and its pictures have been both astounding and humbling. Without the Hubble, it would have been difficult for us to imagine the beauty and wonder that exists beyond our galaxy. By whatever name, this Creative God has watched the continuing evolution of the Universe from the beginning.

It seems reasonable to restrict our conjectures to the one Universe we know, as we could never contact anyone or anything in outside members of a multiverse cosmos. So the second compelling notion is the incomprehensible scale of our Universe. God has had the enormous task, and delight, of keeping intimate track of this creation as it expands. The Hubble, Kepler, and other telescopes have led American astronomers to estimates of a Universe housing some 300 billion galaxies, with 50 trillion stars. God only knows how many planets, and how many more beautiful moons are circling those planets! A recent super-computer simulation in Germany estimated that there are at least *500 billion galaxies* in our Universe. If that *is* the case, increase all those earlier numbers by 66%. In 2011, American astronomers estimated that in our Milky Way galaxy there are more than twice as many planets as there are stars, and estimates of the number of stars in our galaxy run as high as 400 billion. In 2010, we heard that elliptical galaxies may have as many as one trillion stars each, and elliptical galaxies account for about a third of all galaxies. Whatever its true expanse, the Universe is surely large enough to keep its creator occupied and interested.

Third, the Creative Spirit must have enjoyed following all the incredibly different courses that evolution in the natural world has taken throughout the Universe. Because of the huge number of planets, it would also seem highly unlikely that Earth is the only planet with intelligent life on it, notwithstanding that excellent book, *Rare Earth.*[3]

More than 40 years ago, we began listening for radio signal transmissions by thoughtful beings in the Milky Way galaxy, and more recently, far beyond it. On family trips to Boston University's Sargent Camp, near Peterborough, New Hampshire, we would cross over Windy Row Road just to look with awe at the giant disc there, trained to outer space, as part of the "Search for Extraterrestrial Intelligence (SETI)."

Unfortunately, SETI's fiscal woes led to a curtailment of the listening program, but it sprang back into life when NASA's Kepler telescope (now unfortunately defunct) found a planet circling a star similar to our own in a truly *"habitable zone."* Much of the SETI data processing is now being done by informed and dedicated volunteers who allow their computers to be linked via the internet in a vast computational array. Certain spots in the sky seem to produce an unexpectedly large number of radio signals, including static, but as an interesting article noted, *E.T. hasn't called back.*[4] We should keep listening, just in case he does.

Surely there are millions of planets with living things in our own and other galaxies. Our astronomers are finding planets whose physical characteristics are similar to ours, and they have examined only a microscopic part of the Universe. In many of those planets, life will have evolved in mysterious and interesting ways, because evolution hinges on both natural selection and random mutation. That has to be keeping the whole cosmos wonderfully weird. In a Universe as large as ours, it is not likely that Earth's little stage is getting all the best shows.[5]

Fourth, and last: We *"truly modern humans"* made an evolutionary appearance on our little planet only about 200,000 years ago. At some early time, we asserted *free will*, and that was the capstone of keeping the Universe interesting. No chance at all of a boring day for God once his/her creatures decided they knew the difference between right and wrong, and exercised the freedom to choose between them. We don't know if we were the first to have that choice.

We should give the Creative Spirit some much deserved credit. The Universe stems from what can only be seen as a *profoundly* intelligent design, created with an infinite yet almost childlike interest in variation. Siddhartha and Jesus both taught about the holiness of being like children.

TRUTH COMES FIRST.

Our experience of living in the Indian Punjab led us to a great appreciation of the Sikhs, who developed their faith and culture in that northern part of the Indian subcontinent—and equated the Divinity with Truth.

One identifies Sikh men by their beards, their turbans, their height, and their proud demeanor. To me, coming from Abilene, those big wheat-eaters always seemed like West Texans wearing turbans instead of ten-gallon hats. Sikhs say to one another, as a salutation, *"Sat Sri Akal!"* which means *"God's Name Is Truth!"* India is very hard on women, generally, but Sikh women are among the most independent and outspoken in what is largely a heavily patriarchal country

Equating God with Truth is also found in Christianity. For example, students and faculty walking across the campus of the University of Texas can see the inscription from *John* 8:32 carved above the entrance to its Main Building: *"Ye shall know the Truth and the Truth shall make you free."* Paul of Tarsus, who was critical to establishing Christianity as a major world religion, encouraged the little church he had founded in Ephesus to *"put on the whole armor of God!"* He said that the first part of that armor was *truth*. Paul pointedly placed truth before righteousness, peace, faith, salvation, and spirit. Truth came first.

One of the outcomes of our long evolution is that we humans have large brains. It would seem to make sense for us to use those large brains in searching for the truth, even if we don't always agree on its exact nature. To me, science is a deeply religious activity, because its whole purpose is to help us know the truth.

Unlike the late Stephen J. Gould and many others, I don't see science and religion as being in opposition to each other. They do have different methodologies, but they aren't in conflict ideologically. They are both in search of what is real. Everything considered, our growing problem is that for the last 250 years, the scientists have done a substantially better job than the theologians and the preachers.

Most of us noted with great interest when scientists at the super collider in Cern (near Geneva, Switzerland, and strad-dling the border with France) suggested in late 2011 that they had found *intriguing hints* of the Higgs boson. By early 2012 that had moved up to a replicable *bump in their data* and, by 2013, was accepted as fact. The Higgs boson is the elusive *God Particle*, which has been theoretically assigned to have given mass to everything in the Universe, just after the Big Bang.

A member of our family—a scientist and a person of religious conviction—was able to reconcile that discovery with her own belief in God. She was awarded her doctorate in nuclear physics several years ago, and was promptly awarded a post-doctorate to continue her work. Her early interests were in dark matter, which according to current theory makes up some 26% of the Universe. She had worked with a senior research team attempting to weigh an elementary particle called the *neutrino*.

There are several groups of physicists around the world working toward the same goal. The Russians tried to make the world believe that they had determined a neutrino's mass, but their experiment wasn't replicable by other scientists anywhere in the world. Neutrinos travel at near the speed of light. There are so many of them, and they are so small, that while you are reading this sentence, trillions of neutrinos—almost all of them coming from our sun—will pass through your body. They do have some mass, however small.

If and when any of these researchers determine a verifiable mass for one neutrino in an experiment that can be replicated by other scientists, neutrinos will probably account for most of the dark matter in the Universe. The senior research team leaders would then get Nobel Prizes, go home happy, and then, we can hope, join those trying to explain dark energy, which makes up some 69% of the Universe. Everything else—all those 300 to 500 billion galaxies, including our own medium-sized one, of course—makes up a little less than 5% of the Universe.

Our young relative is a deeply religious person. For several years, she and her husband held church in their home for other bright young people, on a regular basis. She once commented that as a teenager, she might have become an atheist. What kept her from that, she said, was the fact that the principles of mathematics—what many call the purest form of truth—pervaded the Universe, uniformly

―――――――

Michael Heller, a professor in Cracow, Poland, was recipient of the 2008 Templeton Prize. Heller is a mathematician and a philosopher. Of late, the Templeton Prize has been about $1.4 million, and is the largest cash prize given annually to a single individual. It is awarded, as they say at the Templeton Foundation, for *"Research or Discoveries about Spiritual Realities."* Heller won the prize primarily for his detailed argument that mathematics offers evidence of God's existence.

After receiving the award, Heller said: *"If we ask about the cause of the Universe, we should also ask about the cause of mathematical laws. By doing so we are back into the great blueprint of God's thinking about the Universe, and the question of ultimate causality: 'Why is there something rather than nothing?'"*

Heller was repeating the excellent question first asked by Gottfried von Leibnitz in 1714 CE. (Jim Holt's intriguing book *Why Does the World Exist?* [2013] is an interesting examination of the many attempts to answer that question.) Among other accomplishments, such as his independent invention of calculus, Leibnitz' work with binary numbers helped make possible our computers, smart phones, and think pads. Thank you, Gottfried!

Leibnitz also coined the doubtful phrase: *"This is the most perfect of all possible worlds!"* At his death, he believed very strongly in a close harmony between the natural world and the God he worshipped. Leibnitz died in 1716, just as science was moving into the forefront of western thought.

According to Plato, who died in 348 BCE, more than 2,000 years before Leibnitz: *"We who are going to talk to one another about the nature of the Universe – how it was created, or how it exists without creation, if we are not altogether out of our wits, must invoke the aid of gods and goddesses, and pray, above all, that our words may be acceptable to them, and thus, acceptable to ourselves."*

Those lines are from *"Timaeus,"* Plato's interesting vision of the Universe. Plato may have been serious in invoking the gods and goddesses of ancient Greece, or he may have been protecting himself from the religious zealots who brought about the death of his teacher, Socrates.

In this book, we are commenting on civilizations that pondered the meaning of existence, and the roles of gods and goddesses, more than 2,500 years before Plato. The American philosopher/historian Will Durant suggested that the Greeks owe more to the Sumerians than we owe to the Greeks.[6] In other words, we also owe a great deal to the Sumerians.

For his day, Will Durant was extraordinarily good on both factual content and ideas. However, some of the dates he cited for Mesopotamia and Egypt are now known to be incorrect. Dating techniques, archaeological findings, and scholarship in related fields have all progressed substantially since his work on early civilization. Much has come to light since then. The advances in science since Durant began his work on civilization are rapidly changing the way we think, act, and believe.

But doesn't science itself require of us some degree of faith if we are to believe in its probabilities? To be meaningful, religion has to live comfortably with the truth, but scientific truth is only one part of our concerns. Equally important is the truth found in those deeply held, widely shared human values on which our civilizations are built. For more than 5,000 years, we have called out for *justice*. We have come to hope and work for social behavior that has long been known as *righteousness*. We have learned that to be human is to know the destructiveness of hate and anger; to be human is to respond to the power of love.

When the Apostle Paul wrote his great paean to love in *1st Corinthians* 13, he included the notion that love rejoices with the truth. At the age of 92, when asked to sum up what he had learned through his life-long service to truth in his study of civilization, Will Durant quoted Jesus from the *Gospel of John* 13:34: *"Love one another,"* and then neatly added a quote from a 19th century Indian philosopher Jiddu Krishnamurti: *"Love is the most practical thing in the world."*

CHAPTER TWO
Leveling the Playing Field

Before going further, we need a common understanding of certain background material related to our history as evolving human beings. As was noted earlier, astronomers now accept the age of the Universe as some 13.8 billion years. That number is based on tests concerning cosmic background microwave radiation that originated with the Big Bang.

Stars in our Milky Way galaxy were among the first to form, so they could be as old as 13.5 billion years, give or take a few million years. As an average-sized galaxy, our Milky Way encompasses some 200-400 billion stars. Our sun is a star that is only about 4.57 billion years old, so our solar system was formed from the debris of older, disintegrated stars in our galaxy. Earth formed shortly after the sun, or about 4.55 billion years ago.

In its early stages, physical evolution on Earth would seem to us to be a very slow process. Bacteria were the first forms of primitive life, and they began to appear in the oceans just over 3.5 billion years ago. Slightly more complex single-celled algae were in the oceans by 3 billion years ago. Plants that we might recognize as such were not in the oceans until some 650 million years ago.

Animals first formed in the ocean, and the fossil remains of those date back some 450 million years. For animals to emerge from the sea and survive on land, there had to be plant cover. The first remains of plants that we might recognize as land-based plants are fossilized spores in rocks in Ireland dating back 475 million years. The first animal fossil remains that we can date come from a millipede found in rocks in Scotland and dating to 428 million years ago.

No evolutionary tale would be complete without the dinosaurs. They first appeared 200 million years ago, and became extinct 60 million years ago, with a few surviving lines such as birds. We humans will have to evolve and mature culturally if we want to last 140 million years. As long as we continue to think that violence is a solution to human problems, our chances of surviving as long as the dinosaurs are near the low end of the probability scale.

On the other hand, those millenialists who think the Rapture is coming soon will be sorely disappointed. Human civilizations rise and fall, but we haven't come to the end of times quite yet, in spite of many such predictions. I liked Martha Gradisher's cartoon that depicted a man coming home wearing a big sandwich board proclaiming—*The End Is Near!* In the caption, his wife asked: *"So should I bother with dinner?"*

Getting dinner has been a problem from the beginning for the hominids, early and late. The timeline for the earliest days of those ape-like, human-like creatures was slowly pushed back by archaeological discoveries in East Africa to 5.5 million years. Then surprisingly, in 2002, in the now-arid West African country of Chad, hominid fossils were found dating back 6.5 million years. It was even possible to determine from the shape of the bones in their fossilized toes that they walked upright. And there was evidence that the area they inhabited was forested.

Most likely, these early hominids came down out of the trees to search for food on the floor of the forest. Later on, their descendants would migrate into the African savanna as the forested areas became too heavily populated for the resources available. Hominids reached Europe about 800,000 years ago, based on a fairly recent archaeological find in Spain.

When did these hominids begin to make stone tools? That date too has been pushed back, to about 2.6 million years ago. To me, this is the first stage of the evolutionary process in which I feel comfortable thinking—*Yes, these really were my ancestors.*

The human DNA molecule was finally decoded in 2001. We know now that genetically we are close kin to those very first tool makers, no matter how primitive they were. Incidentally, their stone tools were dated by studying the magnetic properties of the rocks used in the tools.

Our ancestors may have begun to control and use fire as early as 1.5 million years ago, based on fairly recent finds. This dating was done by examining free radicals in old clay fire pits. The first *Homo sapiens*—*"thoughtful humans"* with large brains—arrived on the earthly scene about 500,000 years ago, but we have to make a distinction between these early humans and ourselves. They were not us.

Some 20 years ago, in a German coal mine in Schoningen, Germany, a set of well-preserved and beautifully balanced wooden spears was found. Based on the soil strata that covered them and other evidence, the *Homo sapiens* who fashioned these long spears lived between 380,000 and 400,000 years ago. But these enterprising spearmakers were not us—their *Homo sapiens* line died out completely.[7]

One of the human groups that followed after them were the Neanderthals—*Homo sapiens Neanderthalis*. They were still around when we truly modern humans arrived in Europe. The last Neanderthal probably died in Spain, only about 28,000 years ago, according to the rather limited fossil record. The *oldest* remains of fully developed Neanderthals date back only some 130,000 years. Our line is a bit older than that.

Although nowadays we like to refer to ourselves as *truly modern humans,* we have classified ourselves, modestly, as *Homo sapiens sapiens*, or *"thoughtful, thoughtful humans."* This stems from our using a spoken language as a part of our survival kit. It also helps that we were the ones doing the talking.

We first appeared in East Africa about 200,000 years ago. Detailed fossilized remains of our ancestors dating to 170,000 years ago have been found in Eritrea and Ethiopia, and some recently found fragments that date as early as 195,000 years ago. Among other things, this means that we co-existed with the Neanderthals over their entire 130,000 year life-span. They are gone, but we survived.

We were *"anatomically modern,"* meaning among other things that we possibly could, but most probably did not speak a language in our earliest years. Most likely, grunts and hand signals were it for a long time. This is still a much debated question.

What happened to the Neanderthals? Best guess: We marginalized them in ways that took away their food supply. Judging from the teeth marks on old bone fragments, there was a significant amount of cannibalism on both sides.

Another question that has caught the attention of those who study our early years is whether or not we were having sex with the Neanderthals. Recent DNA research suggests that there was *reproductive mixing* between the two groups. We all carry Neanderthal genes. For whatever reasons, the Neanderthals didn't make it as a separate human species. We should remember that there were numerous human lines that failed to make the cut. We *"thoughtful, thoughtful humans"* were the only ones who did.

In part, we survived because our larger brains made it possible for us to make better and better stone tools. The literal translation of the terms *Paleolithic* and *Neolithic*, used to distinguish our two prehistoric time periods, is *Old Stone Age* and *New Stone Age*. Of course, the primary difference between them is in the nature of their stone tools.

A major shift in tool-making took place about 12,000 years ago in the Middle East, the area that we are studying. Why then? Because new specially-designed stone tools were needed to assist in doing the new thing—*agriculture.*

So, you may ask, how old is the practice of religion compared to agriculture? Based on archaeological evidence, some anthropologists argue that the Neanderthals had organized religious practices as early as 100,000 years ago: sacred sites, burial of their dead with artifacts, and so on. In one grave site, a Neanderthal family had buried their little daughter with a straw doll and some flowers. We *"truly modern humans"* seem to have taken another 20,000 years or so to get to anything like that level of concern.

In June of 2011, the cover of *National Geographic* magazine headlined the dramatic phrase, *"The Birth of Religion,"* along with a cover to match its subtitle, *"The World's First Temple."* It dealt with the long excavation of Gobekli Tepe, an archaeological site in southeastern Turkey near the border with Syria dating back to 9,600 BCE. The finding of "the oldest known example of monumental architecture" at that location led to the magazine's suggestion that it was the site of the "birth of religion" as well as the "dawn of civilization." As interesting as the site and its contents prove to be, neither of those two suggestions can be accepted comfortably. Perhaps what should have been accentuated more was the *Geographic's* well-presented idea that, most likely, these pre-Stonehenge worshippers of the cosmos were some of the first people to discover and introduce the basic principles of agriculture. The improved food supply that agriculture provided would eventually make it possible to live permanently in a fixed place. But after 2,500 years of nothing but villages, and then 2,000 years of towns, civilization dawns only with the rise of the first city.

So what was the most likely impetus for early religion? A common answer in the literature is "fear of death," but a loving burial with a doll and flowers says more about hope and expectation than it does about fear. In terms of religion's origins, generally, *awe* and *wonder* are strong competitors with fear. Why else would so much of the natural world have been thought to be sacred? Many primitive religions were, and some still are, *animistic*, with the notion that all natural phenomena are innately spiritual. The sun, the moon, and the five "stars" that could be observed to move in the night sky were *deities* in ancient cultures, and that is quite understandable.

We should also mention *dreams* and *reproduction by females*, both of which were great mysteries, and deeply involved in early religious experience. Religion was perhaps the first effort by our ancestors to try to understand their universe, to give structure and meaning to their lives, and to help answer that needling question which keeps popping up in our heads: *Why are we here?*

Throughout the history of mankind, religion and art have closely intertwined with each other and with us. The three illustrations shown below are sculptures widely known as *mother goddesses.* Most were made with an obvious nod to the fertility of the female, which was still a deep and abiding mystery.

The earliest recognizable mother goddess statue was found in the Hohle Fels caves in Germany, and is now being studied at the University of Tubingen.

Figure 2: The Hohle Fels Goddess

Its accomplished sculptor carved it from mammoth ivory some 40,000 years ago. If the figure is not pregnant, it certainly is obese. At that time of chasing down animals and gathering small bits of food, seriously overweight individuals must have been very rare. We may have much to learn on that topic.

The second illustration is of a hand-sized sculpture found near Willendorf, Austria. It is called the *"Willendorf Venus"* and is on display in the Naturhistor-isches Museum in Vienna, Austria. She is probably the best known of the early mother goddess sculptures. Carved out of limestone more than 24,000 years ago, she has the same fleshy features as the goddess from Hohle Fels.

Figure 3: The Willendorf Venus

Lespugue, France was the site for the discovery of a third mother goddess. She was carved from mammoth ivory and is about 25,000 years old. (Artist friends believe this sculptor could make a good living today!) The Venus of Lespugue is in the Musée de l'Homme in Paris.

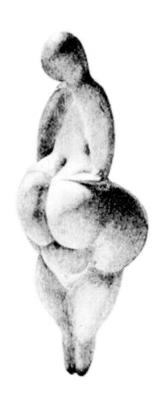

Figure 4: The Venus of Lespugue
(Based on a reconstruction from six pieces)

Archaeological evidence suggests that the mother goddess was a central part of early religion long before agriculture, widespread settlement in villages, or the development of towns. These archaeological finds suggest that goddess worship stems from a time when men had little or no idea of their role in human reproduction.

A pregnant female was a mystery and a wonder. That didn't stop a few early carvers from sculpting the erect male phallus. Almost certainly that was an indication they enjoyed sex, not that they understood the relationship of the penis to pregnancy. These carvings may just have been the first sex toys. An early one was found in Hohl Fels cave, in Germany, where the oldest-known Mother Goddess was uncovered.

As I mentioned earlier, religion based on human images was not the earliest form of spiritual belief. Animism is older. Our word for it stems from *anima*, Latin for *soul*. Humans were in touch with, and dependent on, all forms of material—animal, vegetable, and mineral. To believe that all material forms had souls suggests that the soul was a universal spirit. Because early humans had no written language, we depend on the artifacts they made to suggest what they might have believed. This is a bit risky.

One of the best of the early sculptural finds is a little horse carved out of mammoth ivory. It was found in a cave near Vogelherd, Germany, and dates back at least 30,000 years.

Figure 5: The Vogelherd Horse

This remarkable sculpture may have been a talisman carried by a hunter to help in finding horses for food—there are two carved notches on it. The sculpture may very well have played a part in worshipping horses, generally. Of course, there is always the chance that the sculptor just appreciated horses.

That may have been the case as well for almost all the early cave *painters*, who chose to depict horses more than any other animal. At any rate, the study of bones in ancient caves, including the Hohle Fels cave, suggests that horse meat was not their favorite meal. There were many more bones from animals such as reindeer, antelope, deer, and bison.

Cave paintings are among our oldest artistic endeavors. In Europe, the best of these range from an estimated 33,000 to 10,000 years ago. For more than 20,000 years, a rather strict format was followed for painting animals on cave walls. Some scholars believe there may even have been itinerant artists who traveled widely, giving lessons in cave painting.

Certain anthropologists think that cave paintings reflect a kind of religious entreaty for success by the artists or their tribes as hunters, and often use the term *sympathetic magic*. Recent work by Dean Snow, an anthropologist at Pennsylvania State University, suggests that many, if not most, of the cave artists were women, based on the comparative hand sizes of the artists.[?] Snow has studied the hand prints surrounding the horses painted 25,000 years ago in Peche Merle cave in southern France, among other sites. In those pre-historic times, hunting was largely a male activity, but painted inspiration by women is an interesting possibility.

Figure 6: Hands and horses in the Peche Merle cave

Figure 7: Reindeer in Font de Gaume, 14,000 BCE

For the most part, our Cro-Magnon ancestors in Europe ate reindeer, but were inspired to paint horses. Worldwide, some 42% of all cave painting figures are horses, and in Europe, over 50%. Some of the best were among the earliest—painted in the Chauvet cave in southern France, beginning some 32,000 years ago.

Figure 8: *"Shaded Horses"* from the Chauvet cave

Also in that cave are paintings of rhinoceros, lions, and reindeer, which suggests something interesting about the range of climate in that day. Southern France was like southern Scandinavia, but with a tropical touch.

Cave paintings around the world express the spirit of the subjects depicted, and humans were among those subjects. The expressions of spirit are in the paintings. There were no written words to tell us about their faith.

People can't live on faith alone, so we need to know how we got to bakeries in cities. It is very important for us to understand how cities came to be if we are to understand how civilization and scriptures for organized religion came to be. It turns out that our ability to use language played a major role in the development of cities. We also need to know that women made five game-changing contributions which shaped our path toward civilization.

CHAPTER THREE
The Early Years:
Roles and Responsibilities

Physical anthropologists believe that some 65,000 years ago, we were using an early form of language—a proto-language, if you will. The major language groups in use on earth today were all well on their way to formation by 50,000 years ago. The separation of people into tribal groups inside the great language groups led to the development of individual languages.

This is a good time to point out that tribes tended to form around a group of families who believed they had a common ancestor, often mythical, but sometimes real. It is not surprising that they would remain closely connected through that belief and the language they spoke in common.

Inside the Semitic language group were languages with such familiar names as Arabic, Aramaic, Egyptian, and Hebrew, but there were also less familiar ones such as Akkadian, Canaanite, Ugaritic, Amorite, and Eblaite. Also, in the ancient Middle East, there were a number of languages that fell outside any known language group, and Sumerian is a good example of such languages with no traceable links.[9]

Except possibly for the Americas, all the major habitable land masses were being settled by 30,000 years ago. Some archaeologists suggest that Asian immigrants came to South America by sea about 30,000 years ago, but recent and wide-spread DNA testing in that continent doesn't give much support to such a notion. That battle is still being waged.

Archaeological and genetic evidence in and around the state of Pennsylvania does suggest that immigrants of European origin were there from about 19,000 years ago. They eventually mixed in with our Native American immigrants who began walking in from East Asia across the land bridge to Alaska, beginning some 13,000-plus years ago. That was during the last Ice Age when sea levels in the Pacific Ocean had fallen by 325 feet, leaving the Bering Straits high and dry. Most of the early Americans made the trek over that connecting link.

Across the Atlantic, our European ancestors were thriving, even in the harsh conditions of the last Ice Age. Early archae-ologists called them the Cro-Magnon people, but they were just our *Homo sapiens sapiens* relatives. They made warmer clothing out of animal skins, and made new and better weapons for killing large animals, including the largest around, the mammoth. In fact, we truly modern humans finally hunted mammoths to extinction. In North America, there has been a meaningful correspondence between findings of mammoth bones and fluted spear points, one of the new technologies of the early Americans.

As the earth finally warmed up from its deep freeze and the ice melted, there were dramatic changes on the earth: rising sea levels, huge new rivers, thousands of new lakes, and the development of new vegetative cover where before there had been only scoured earth and glacial debris. For the purposes of this story, and all of this is our story and our history, we need to know about some specific changes that took place in the Middle East.

These changes began to occur about 14,000 years ago. Prior to that time, the valleys of the Nile and the Tigris and Euphrates were all very, very wet. In fact, they were basically inhospitable swamps. Over the course of some 2,000 years, these swamps turned into deserts and steppes—but very special kinds of deserts and steppes.

They were special because they still had great rivers flowing through them, with fertile alluvial soil along their banks and relatively long growing seasons. They were to become, over time, productive agricultural sites once people developed ways to irrigate the land using water from the river, from shallow wells, or from managed seasonal flooding, as in the lower Nile valley and along the Euphrates.

Before these climatic changes occurred, life was difficult in almost all parts of the world. Most people who survived early childhood died in their twenties and thirties, and a 40-year-old was a senior citizen. But if you were one of the few who were genetically and physically strong enough to reach age 50, there was a good chance you might live another decade or more as a real elder in your tribe.

From the arrival of truly modern humans, a basic division of labor developed: men hunted and women gathered. The men were hunting medium-to-large animals mostly. The women were engaged primarily in gathering products from plants: edible leaves, roots, and bark; and all kinds of seeds, including wild grass seeds, as well as nuts, berries, and other fruit. They also caught fish and other small animals, including insects, for food.

The division of labor into men as hunters and women as gatherers led to a fundamental difference in their territorial needs: Men always needed to move on, as they were hunting game that was not only mobile, it could be depleted. In most locations, if you wanted meat, you had to keep going.

Women, who traded sex for meat, bore the children. They needed more time in one place. Gathering, especially of wild grass seeds, was a time-consuming activity. In the course of thousands of years of experience in these roles, women learned a great deal and passed that knowledge down to each successive generation.

This became much easier with the full development of language. Women could transmit what they knew orally as well as by example. But they had to do all this while still young by modern standards, because life expectancy for most was so short.

This is a good time to note that for at least the last 50,000 years, language has been our primary means of transmitting human culture. For the 150,000 years before that, imitative behavior had been the dominant means of communication. Today, worldwide, the complex experience of living in cities is a very important and still growing means of transmitting culture. (We haven't even reached the first city in our story, however. We will get there shortly.)

Let us look at some of the key early cultural changes based on contributions most likely made by women:

First, as an outcome of their experience and knowledge of plants, women discovered the basic principles of agriculture. Possibly they remembered spilling some grass seeds near a spring, and when they came back later, after a period of warm weather, there were the full grown plants. Something of this sort may have happened many times in many places before full comprehension set in.

The basic, practical requirements of growing grain were probably known by a few small groups in the Middle East beginning about 14,000 years ago. In that area, agriculture, with new and appropriate stone tools, was well-developed and spreading by 12,000 years ago. Again, new stone tools for agriculture mark the transition to the Neolithic Era from the more primitive, less specialized Paleolithic.

Archaeological finds suggest that a hardy strain of barley was domesticated first, followed by two types of wheat, *einkorn* and *emmer*, in the high meadows or upland valleys of the area we now know as Iraq, Iran, and eastern Turkey. Note that this was not in the lowlands, but up at higher elevations, away from the river valleys.

One of those two wheat varieties, *emmer*, didn't "shatter" or shed its seeds as easily as the other, so it became the preferred variety. You could gather it easily. But if you wanted to consume emmer wheat on a larger scale, you had to plant it since it couldn't scatter its own seeds.

Over the long haul, barley became the most important grain in Mesopotamia because it could tolerate poor soil. Soil fertility declines with prolonged use of the land and with increased salinity brought about from irrigating in desert soils. Barley could tolerate this poorer soil, but wheat was the desired crop, if it could be grown.

Early farmers learned a great deal more than collecting seeds, digging holes, planting and covering seeds, and watering them. They learned how to cross-breed varieties to get improved strains, how to transplant crops and how to graft fruit trees. Originally, anything that dealt with plants was the responsibility of women. However, once a community began to depend on agriculture, the men began hunting less and less, or not at all, and the crop's survival meant the community's survival. Everyone was involved, and both men and women contributed to agriculture's development.

Men are generally credited with the invention of the plow, simply because it required a substantial amount of upper-body strength to guide one. The plow was much more than a labor saving device. Turning over the soil directly increased productivity by bringing nutrients into the root zone of plants.

Men would always defend the crop from outsiders, usually with weapons they made themselves. But there was an even bigger challenge than hungry marauders—men had to help women find ways to keep the soil moist so plants would grow to maturity. Men and women dug whatever earthworks were necessary to develop a relatively permanent source of water. Those included wells, ditches, canals, water lifts of all kinds, storage basins, and so on. In the rural areas of the developing world today, men and women often worked together on such tasks, typically with the men digging and the women carrying away dirt in baskets.

Women must have been quite willing to participate in these irrigation projects, because carrying water for plants was almost certainly their responsibility, too. In poor countries today, carrying water is a task that is seldom done by men, but women do it routinely. Men do work a variety of devices designed to lift water, but women do most of the water carrying, unless a motorized vehicle can be involved. With that addition, the men get interested.

Second, now that a harvest could produce more food than a group could eat in a few sittings, women began to make more and better containers. Surplus food needed to be stored, carried and protected. At first women made baskets out of materials they already knew well: reeds, vines and bark. And then, in a great leap forward, someone made pots out of clay—pots that could easily be sealed to keep out moisture, insects, rats, and so on. With a sealed pot, you could reasonably ensure a safe supply of seeds for next year's planting.

Some of the oldest known pottery has a basket-like look to it, from pressing the outside with mats or ropes. And that suggests that women were the makers of these early pots, as they had been the early basket makers. At any rate, the makers liked the look of a basket more than they liked the look of a plain clay pot. Of course, over time, pottery-making would lead to major artistic accomplishments by both men and women. Much later, men would dominate the mass-production of pottery, as a very steady source of income.

A third contribution by women came from their moving from the weaving of baskets to the weaving of materials for clothing. Of course, this eventually led to the spinning of plant and animal fibers into thread and the production of clothing that was much lighter than animal skins. Animal skins were probably harder to come by, too, wherever farming took precedence over hunting.

A fourth, enormously important contribution by women was their gradual development of pharmacological medicine. This was a natural by-product of their ever-growing knowledge of plants. Over a long period of time, women created this very meaningful way to support the health of their families.

Of course, in much of the world today, including China, India and the Middle East, people still rely heavily on herbal medicine, and it plays an increasingly significant role in the growing practice of holistic medicine in Western culture. Plants still play a key underlying role even in the modern pharmaceutical industry, with perhaps a third of all modern medicine based on plants.[10]

A fifth contribution attributable primarily to women is that of animal domestication. The long process likely began when men brought baby animals back to camp after their hunting trips, or when women found baby animals while gathering. That made an enormous impact on human food supply and the lives of early people. The need to have a continuous supply of such animals eventually led to efforts to reproduce these animals intentionally. To do that, one had to understand the roles of both males and females. The mystery of the fertile woman began to fade, and the worship of male gods and the phallus became commonplace.

There is some recent argument as to whether the first animals to be domesticated were dogs. Dogs must have been among the earliest, probably first for food and then for company. Men quickly became interested in dogs when they noticed two other canine characteristics: they had useful hunting instincts, and were fiercely protective.

Gradually, grass-eating animals such as goats, sheep, and cattle were domesticated, giving an important boost to the food supply through access to milk and more readily available meat. Cattle, oxen, and water buffalo were the true prizes, because they were strong enough to pull plows.[11]

If you had them, you wanted to keep your cattle, oxen, and water buffalo alive as long as possible; but when they died, or were killed for meat, the hides were a major benefit also. Scavengers such as chickens and pigs made an easy entry into our early world.

Up to this point, one might think that human societies would have had a better-than-average chance of developing as matriarchal societies, in which the female role—the *Female Principle*—was dominant. And that must have been the case, for both agricultural and non-agricultural societies in early days. Earth/Mother Goddess worship seems likely to have been a primary religious focus for much of the past 50,000 years.[12]

That became a very different story for the groups that took advantage of the domestication of animals to develop nomadic herding. Nomadic herding is a fairly recent development, coming on the scene about 6,500 years ago when the first agricultural areas became overpopulated. In a very real sense, much of the arid and semi-arid world eventually split between the agriculturalists and the animal herders—between the farmers and the shepherds.[13]

In animal herding, male upper-body strength was needed to herd, corral, and slaughter large animals, dress carcasses and, where cattle were involved, castrate young bulls. Of course, nomadic herding required a thorough, practical understanding of the male role in reproduction. That understanding developed in early villages that kept animals for plowing. All of this helped bring about the loss of that early centrality women enjoyed in religion.

Men introduced the worship of bulls and their large genitalia. They even began to worship the human phallus. The Male Principle was promoted, and that led to dominance by male gods and a patriarchal legacy that has unbalanced civilization for many centuries.

My own reading suggests that women in early Sumeria were treated well, but never given preferential treatment over men. As patriarchal groups took charge, they displaced many goddesses with gods, even creating new myths in which male gods killed goddesses. Women were treated more harshly than men, particularly in regard to harsher punishment for the same crime, unequal rules for giving evidence and testimony, lower wages for the same work, etc. Unequal treatment became codified under laws that favored men.

The need for muscle strength to handle animals and frequent fighting with other nomadic groups over territory were only two of the factors that helped push nomadic groups to develop male-dominated societies. Many became strictly patriarchal. Keep in mind that many early Semitic people, such as the Arabs, the Hebrews, and the Akkadians, were both nomadic and patriarchal.

We will return to the role of gender discrimination later because it played an important part in early religion and civilization, and it is important today. As long as fundamentalism remains a factor in any world religion, gender issues will continue to be near the front of human concerns. The comparative historian Arnold Toynbee suggested that it will take another 2,000 years to iron out the main conflicts in world religion. We should all hope it doesn't take that long to give women their basic human rights.

Back to those early contributions by women: *agriculture, containers, weaving and spinning, pharmacological medicine,* and *animal domestication*. These, plus that major invention by men, the plow, made it possible for human groups to settle down in villages.

There were some villages even before the invention of agriculture. They developed around those rare places that had a very reliable food supply. Such sites included coastal locations where fish could be caught easily most of the year, along bays where shellfish were virtually unlimited, and anywhere animals congregated for any reason. The latter included locations near breeding grounds for ducks and geese, like some stone villages found in Siberia that were built nearly 100,000 years ago. There were also villages built along the great migration routes for bison, elk, caribou, and reindeer. At all of these sites, food could be easily obtained and at least semi-permanent settlements could be maintained.

The development of agriculture opened up a vast new territory for fixed human settlement in villages. In these early agricultural villages, food surpluses developed gradually. Over time, those surpluses became more reliable. That offered the possibility of a whole range of larger communities which were not strictly rural or agricultural, like villages, but were genuinely *urban* in nature. There, some of the local folk could earn a living without any direct participation in farming. This marked a major milestone in human history.

CHAPTER FOUR
The Rise of Cities

Wherever substantial food surpluses from nearby villages were stable, towns were possible. Many people could earn a living at something other than plowing, planting, or harvesting. Towns began to develop sometime after 9,000 BCE. Most old town sites, such as Jericho, have underlying strata of debris accumulated when the site was just a village.

Jericho, on the west bank of the Jordan River valley in Canaan, may have been the earliest town. Others, perhaps as old, include Jarmo, near what is now the Iranian border with Iraq, and Catal Huyuk in southeastern Turkey. Catal Huyuk was probably three times as large as Jericho or Jarmo, and was the most advanced town in the Neolithic era. It wasn't a city, even though some authors suggest that it was that complex.

A thriving town had many things besides an adequate food supply and some specialized non-rural jobs. For example, in Catal Huyuk, there were home altars, with mother goddesses and cattle as a focus for their religion. Thirty mother-goddess statuettes have been found there.

After the British archaeologist James Mellaart excavated Catal Huyuk extensively in 1961, he suggested that the religion of this early Neolithic town had most likely been established by women.[14] That generated a substantial controversy, as his reasoning was that the art and artifacts did not display the usual degree of vulgarity exhibited in sites known to be male-dominated.

Those of you who have visited the extraordinary Pre-Hittite Museum in Ankara, Turkey, probably remember a seated mother-goddess statue flanked by two leopards. It was one of those found at Catal Huyuk.

Figure 9: Seated Mother Goddess, Catal Huyuk

The walls of 33 of the homes at Catal Huyuk had decorative art. Six of those were paintings of a distant snow-capped mountain, now called Mt. Hasandagi. One of the more interesting wall paintings at Catal Huyuk was done perhaps 7,000 years ago. This wall painting is described in some of the archaeological literature only as a collection of deer-hunting scenes, but Picasso was probably correct in his observation that the early painters knew everything there was to know about art.

Figure 10: Wall painting at Catal Huyuk

For Catal Huyuk, or any other early town, one of the important questions is what led to the transformation of a village into a town. Other than that there was enough food to support a growing population, and demand for a variety of non-agricultural products and services, the answer is most often trade—trade with other places.

Trade may have had its origins in the old migratory urge of male hunters, or it may have started simply as a way for some curious people to find out about more of the world. At any rate, it was one way for some folks, mostly men, to earn a living by hitting the road and trading something. And of course, ideas went along with trade, in both directions.

What did these early towns trade? Many things, but these trade items were determined not only by a particular town's agricultural accumulations, but also by its nearby resource base. Everything depended on finding or making something locally that others wanted or needed. Five things stand out in the trade of early towns.

The first and second are directly related to agriculture: *surplus grain* and *surplus animals*. Surplus grain meant that after the villages around a town had saved sufficient seed grain for next year's crop, and after they had stored the grain needed to survive the coming year, there was still grain left over to sell or trade.

Any such surplus was commonly exchanged by towns with other towns and, of course, with villages just outside the purview of the community with the surplus food. Surplus animals could be walked and sold or traded to nearby communities that needed them, but as towns flourished and populations grew, animals and grain were imported for food, not exported.

The third trade item was food-related, and that was *surplus salt*. Saline springs in Europe and China have been used as a source for salt over the past 8,000 years. In rare cases, the salt might come from mines working underground salt deposits, but early on, people learned to evaporate sea water or water from salt springs and salt lakes to retain the salt, or to scrape salt off salt flats in the desert. Then, they would trade it to groups of people that had no salt. As a condiment and food preservative, salt was highly prized. It could cure meat, and that was an important early discovery.

The fourth item was quite significant in trade between towns, and was often traded over great distances. It consisted of a variety of *cutting tools*, mostly for domestic use, but also for use as weapons. By far the most commonly traded items were flint blades, and flint is often referred to in the world's early commercial records. But the top of the line leather-cutting tool of the day was the black volcanic glass we know as obsidian. Flaked obsidian was exceptionally sharp, *so* users had to box it in some way, around pieces of wood, to avoid cutting their hands before they cut the leather.

Research chemists today can determine the place of origin of a piece of obsidian by examining its chemical composition and crystalline structure. Nearby obsidian was at the heart of the prosperity of Catal Huyuk. Obsidian from outcrops near that early town in southeast Turkey have been found in archaeological sites all around the Mediterranean coast, and far inland in the Middle East. A good piece of obsidian was a prized possession. Later on, metal knives would take over, but for many centuries, obsidian was a major item of trade.

You may have been to the great surface outcrop of obsidian near Bend, Oregon, in an old volcanic area. Steel walkways have been constructed so you can climb to the top of this shiny black hill, but every walkway has a prominently displayed sign: "STAY ON THE METAL STAIRS! THE OBSIDIAN WILL CUT THROUGH YOUR SHOES!" Well, cutting leather was what made obsidian famous.

There was another important use of obsidian. In a fairly large flake of this volcanic glass, you could see your reflection. Its use as a mirror added to obsidian's value as a trade item. Ten different women were buried at Catal Huyuk with their obsidian mirrors.[15] And that leads us to the fifth group of major trade items—*objects of beauty*.

Included were polished stones, particularly amber and jade, gold, silver, copper, and later on, bronze. One could trade any bright, colorful, intrinsically beautiful or shiny thing from which jewelry could be made. Vanity is a very old vice, and raw materials and finished jewelry were traded far from their sources for use by men and women.

As mentioned earlier, certain villages developed into towns about 9,000 years ago, or around 7,000 BCE. After about 2,000 years, around 5,000 BCE, a few well-favored towns made prosperous through trade began to evolve into a new creation—*cities*. Compared to a town, a city was obviously larger in both area and population, but it was a very different kind of urban community.

Cities devoted resources to monumental building projects, with temples, palaces, granaries, public baths, wide streets, and enduring art to match. Cities supported many types of specialized artisans unknown to towns. What led cities to this dramatic transformation, other than their prosperity from trade?

As we shall see in the next chapter, there were 10 important factors driving the transformation from towns to cities, from cities to civilization. For the most part, they were spelled out for us nearly 100 years ago by Will Durant, in his epic telling of the story of civilization.[16] The first volume of that effort, published in 1935, gave me a foundation for understanding the origin of cities.

There are many other excellent books that introduce the material presented here, but not all are easily accessible. Some try to suggest that although the ideas and beliefs of ancient civilizations may have been borrowed by the writers of the Old Testament, there was no moral underpinning in those early societies. That is not true. This small volume is a summary of the main ideas I found from reading such books, but the final assumptions as to what occurred, and why, are mine.

CHAPTER FIVE

The Ubaid, the Sumerians, and the First Civilization

Cities developed first in *Mesopotamia*, Greek for *"land between the rivers."* Those rivers were the Tigris and the Euphrates. The first city on our planet was named Eridu, and it was founded about 5,100 BCE, in what is now southern Iraq.

Eridu was built by a people known as the Ubaid, named after a site where their pottery was first uncovered. The Ubaid may have been early (prehistoric) Sumerians, but because they had no written language when Eridu was built, no one knows for certain. However, when the Sumerians began to write, one of their first efforts was to compose a King List that stretched back 2,000 years. It began with the king of Eridu.

One ancient cuneiform tablet suggests that there were at least 100 Sumerian cities, but most likely that included a large number of centers that were properly towns. Today, some archaeologists list 40 or more Sumerian cities, others list only 28. In any case, Sumeria was the world's first civilization—an increasingly complex urban society with widely shared values. What made this possible? Sumerian civilization was the outcome of 10 technical and intellectual achievements that were in place by about 3300 BCE.

The first of these, and the foundation of the others, was a highly productive grain-animal agricultural system. Agriculture had first developed in upland valleys nearby. Descendants of those early farmers and some of their neighbors, who had also learned to cultivate grain, moved down to the great fertile plains of the Tigris-Euphrates River system. It is possible that some of the earliest of these farmers were driven out of their high valleys by the last of the mini-ice ages. The timing is about right. These new arrivals were the forerunners of the Ubaid people who built Eridu, the first city.

Based on barley and wheat varieties very similar to those we grow today, the Sumerians developed an agricultural system that could support large concentrations of people. By 3,000 BCE, the farmers were cultivating with an ox-drawn plow, and a few plowshares of the more advanced landowners were coated with copper or bronze. Using reeds similar in size to bamboo, the Sumerians had invented tubular seed drills, which they attached just behind the plow, centered over the new row being formed by the plow.

Seed drills are one of the great tools of efficient, productive farming. With a seed drill, a farmer can drop seeds into the tube at exactly the rate and spacing required for a particular crop while plowing, without bending down to the ground.[17]

Second, the Sumerians had developed irrigation canals to support their agriculture, and local officials were responsible for maintaining those canals. Successful agriculture and the cities it fed were only made possible because the Sumerians knew how to plan, dig, and maintain gravity-fed irrigation canals coming off the Tigris-Euphrates river system.

For generations, this ensured an environment favorable to healthy crops: fertile soil, abundant sunshine, and water available whenever the plants needed it and applied in the correct amounts. After many years of annual cultivation, salt working upward in the soil became a major problem, but not as much when the cities were young.

Annual flooding early in the year from both the Tigris and Euphrates dropped fertilizing silt particularly along the lower courses of the rivers. A bad year for Sumerian agriculture was more likely to be the result of excessive flooding rather than from drought. Unfortunately for the settlers in Mesopotamia, the Tigris and Euphrates *were* prone to destructive floods, which made for an uneasy existence in Sumerian society.

Third, the invention of the potter's wheel led to the development of wheeled carts and the improvement of roads. Around 3500 BCE, the wheel and the potter's wheel both appeared in Mesopotamia. The idea of the wheel may possibly have been an import, but even so, the potter's wheel was invented in the old city of Susa (biblical "Sushan").

Susa was a Ubaid/Sumerian trading outpost up on the Iranian plateau. It had been created as a way-station to modern-day Afghanistan by Ubaid traders from their second-oldest city, Uruk. In Afghanistan, one could trade for local gem stones, or, more importantly, for a variety of goods brought there from India including gems, spices, and textiles.

Sumerians' knowledge of the wheel led to the development and extensive use of wheeled carts. These carts were for hauling crops, delivering trade goods, or whatever that might be pushed by hand. Then the Sumerians increased trade over longer distances by inventing and using ox-drawn vehicles. That brought about investment in an extensive road system between cities, encouraging a growing trading network. However, rivers remained the main avenues for trade. All the wood and stone used in Sumerian cities came from forests and quarries along the major rivers, but those sites were very far upstream.

Fourth, boats had been around for thousands of years, but the Sumerians invented a sailboat which they waterproofed with pitch, found in natural outcrops in the upper reaches of the Tigris. This gave the Sumerians enormous savings in animal and human energy, and provided a much wider range of navigation. A sailboat carrying cargo upstream still managed to move freight about twice as fast as donkeys or oxcarts on roads. With favorable river conditions, cargo coming downstream moved steadily and swiftly, with little need for sails.

With sails and waterproofing, Sumerian boats could now go beyond the river delta and venture out along the coastline, in whatever direction they chose. Before long, Sumerian merchants were trading directly with areas that we now know as India and Pakistan. Sumerian jewelry has been found in ancient graves in the interior of southern India, well beyond the mountains that border the western coast.

Fifth, the Sumerians' Ubaid predecessors had invented a loom for making cloth. The Sumerians improved it by adding a draw shuttle to feed thread rapidly across the loom. The result was better-quality cloth woven at a faster rate. Also, now it was possible to introduce more elaborate designs. Not only did the Sumerians make cloth, they wove rugs and made tapestry-like wall hangings—a relatively sophisticated textile art form developed in Sumeria.

Sixth, recent scholarship points to the Ubaid people (or their close neighbors) as those who developed the complex processes of metallurgy in the early sixth millennium, BCE.[18] The Sumerians improved on the technology by inventing and using the lost-wax process for casting. This copper and bronze metallurgy meant more items to use, enjoy, and trade. It also provided new weapons for waging war. Unfortunately, war most often meant one Sumerian city attacking another—this early society's greatest flaw.

Seventh, the Sumerians had developed and were using abstract mathematics, including both algebra and geometry. The Sumerians made use of square roots and cube roots, and discovered the Pythagorean Theorem almost two thousand years before Pythagoras.

In popular cultural practice, apparently stemming from a much earlier time with a different counting system, there was an affinity for numbers based on six. From the Sumerians we get our 60 seconds (6 x 10) in a minute, 60 minutes (6 x 10) in an hour, and two blocks of 12 hours (6 x 2) to make a 24-hour (6 x 4) day. (Incidentally, the Sumerians also invented the sundial. The Egyptians borrowed it from them and made improvements.)

Sumerian mythology had two creation stories, and both made their way into the Old Testament 2,000 years later. In one of those, a deity created the Universe and everything in it in six days by *naming the names*. One major step was accomplished each day for six days, just as in the story borrowed for *Genesis*. The seventh day was to be a day of rest—but unlike

Genesis, not so God could rest—that would have been an irreverent suggestion to an all-powerful creator.

Although the people did get to rest on the seventh day, that was not the main point, either. After all, people had been created by a powerful deity so that lesser gods and goddesses would not have to work. People were to worship the divine on that seventh day, as *Genesis* would make clear much later. Worship isn't supposed to make you tired.

In one of the Sumerians' creation stories, rest on the seventh day was specifically directed so that your ox could recuperate from plowing the fields. The writers of the Hebrew bible had many centuries of oral history in which to improve the Sumerian story. Their version in *Genesis* was more poetic, more generous in spirit, and still provided a day off for your ox.

Eighth, Sumerian builders used a number of innovations, including ladders, pulleys, levers, and hinges. More importantly, their architects made use of the column, the arch, the vault, and the dome. (A vault is a roof or ceiling in the form of an arch, and a dome is a hemispherical vault.) All of these were used in building Sumerian palaces and granaries, and so on, and were the architectural base for most of the world's public buildings for the next 5,000 years.

Ninth, the Sumerians, and almost certainly others before them, had carefully observed the movement of the stars for hundreds of years, and speculated openly about the meaning of the cosmos. One of the outcomes of those observations was a reasonably serviceable 12-month lunar calendar. Each month had 30 days (6 x 5), so the calendar was a little short. Accordingly, every sixth year, they added a 13th month to correct it, more or less. Of course they knew the sun and the moon, but they also knew Sumerian names for the five planets that moved in the night sky: Mercury, Venus, Mars, Jupiter, and Saturn.[19]

From this important cosmic set of seven—the sun, moon, and those five visible planets—came a new and abiding interest in the number seven. All seven were regarded as deities, and we still recognize all seven, directly or indirectly, in the names we use for our seven days of the week. In a natural merging of their astronomy and mythology, the Sumerians came to see (and illustrate them) as their *Tree of Life*, with the sun god as the trunk, and the other six as branches off the trunk, reaching to the sky.

Tenth, and most important of all, the Sumerians were the first people to have a written language. This evolved naturally enough from the Sumerian preoccupation with keeping records of their trade transactions. Scribes developed a cuneiform[20] script that began with simple pictographs, and then grew into a syllabic writing system.

One of the oldest letters ever found in Sumeria was written in cuneiform script on a clay tablet, and has a familiar ring to it. The letter was from one scribe to another. It is on one of the more than two million cuneiform tablets that have been uncovered in this broad cultural area. In that letter, the scribe expressed his distress to a colleague over the behavior of his teen age son, who won't keep up his work at the local school for scribes.

The letter says: *I've told my son that he doesn't have to help out with the work on our farm, or even help with the chores here in town, if he will just do well in school! But he won't do it—all he wants to do is go down town and hang out with his friends!*

Well, the father actually wrote something closer to *meet his friends,* but we understand the situation. The letter was written more than 4,000 years ago.

This parental complaint may have been heartfelt, but a response by a student scribe was so popular among his cohorts that a number of nearly identical clay tablet copies have been found in various parts of Sumeria. The complaint is that the teacher is not a good person, at all.

Basically, the responding student's message was this:

> *I was beaten four times yesterday, once when the schoolmaster said my work wasn't correct, but it was, so I ran off. They caught me downtown, and I was beaten again. Then the schoolmaster complained about my speaking to a friend near the end of the day, and I was*

beaten for the third time. Then I was beaten at home, by my father. If he would only do what the other fathers do—give the schoolmaster a big meal and a gift—I wouldn't have any problems at school!

So the father finally invites the teacher over for dinner, and gives him a nice robe and a ring. Sure enough, the son begins to receive good marks at the school for scribes. One teller of the story even had the schoolmaster sending a nice note to the father saying, in effect: *It is remarkable how much your son has improved!*

———

We noted earlier that, with the development of cities, there were massive construction projects: temples, palaces, granaries, public baths, roads, canals, walls for defending the city, and more. These large-scale projects also meant large-scale spending, and some form of taxation to match. Deficit financing wasn't possible, so the people had to pay up front, in one form or another. An old Sumerian proverb said: *"You may have a lord, and you may have a king, but the man to fear is the tax collector."*

On the other hand, there was a great deal more wealth and leisure for the upper classes: the ruling families (the nobility of the day), the military elite, the priesthood, and merchants with large-scale enterprises. Public baths were also provided, and public gardens made the city more attractive for all. While the people produced more and made more technological advances, there was a continuing threat: war with another city.

Violence, even invasion, was nothing new to the first city, Eridu, but aggressive war as a policy option evolved rather quickly after a larger set of cities was established. A city's defined limits set both the immediate agricultural base and the taxable limits for a city ruler, so disputes over boundaries were among the first causes of wars. Also, other cities were attractive targets for any city already in distress. A nearby, more prosperous city would possess a variety of valuable goods—not the least of which would be food.

Men had always been ready to defend their families, then their villages, then their towns, and now their cities. But this new thing, war for advantage, meant that your city's leaders could call on you to attack a neighboring city that posed no real threat. Unfortunately, cooperation and sharing were survival tactics for only a few enlightened city-state leaders.

Later on, emperors who had conquered large numbers of cities would force their cooperation, requiring them to share resources—either through harsh confiscation or a straightforward redistribution of whatever was available. The form and amount of forced sharing of resources depended on the ruler and all the pertinent circumstances—especially who had supported whom in the last conflict.

Today, this area we came to know as Sumeria is in southern Iraq. As the home of the first civilization, it had once defined greatness. For a very long time, the West did not even know that Sumeria had ever existed. What little remained of it had been destroyed by the Persians and the Parthians by 350 BCE. After that, wind-borne sand covered up most of the remaining traces of the cities of Sumeria. What could be seen were a few scraggly remnants of ancient stair-stepped temples, and many mounds of urban debris covered with sand. The bulk of each debris pile was mud brick.

Understandably, Western scholars assumed that these mounds were old Assyrian or Babylonian ruins—civilizations they knew about. On their maps, Muslim cartographers identified each mound as a particular *Tell*, which means *mound* in Arabic. Some initial discoveries, recognized as city ruins belonging to a civilization even older than Babylonia, were made in the late 1700s.

There were a few more such discoveries in the early 1800s, then major advances were made in the 1840s. Many more ruins were found all over Mesopotamia and in neighboring areas as the 19th Century played out. This process of discovery went on sporadically throughout the 20th Century, between wars involving that region.

From the very first, great quantities of clay tablets were uncovered, but many were broken. Most of these tablets were covered with cuneiform writing, produced by punching the tablets with a wedge-shaped stylus when the clay was soft. Some 25,000 are still excavated every year, often in areas as far away as Lebanon, Israel, Jordan, Syria, Turkey, and Iran. The total found is well over two million.

The Archaeological Museum in Istanbul has some 100,000 cuneiform tablets, many of which have not yet been translated. All of those were found in urban debris mounds in Turkey. Most of the eastern half of Turkey was a part of the Mesopotamian culture area.

The British Museum has more than 120,000 cuneiform tablets, from 22 major sites in Mesopotamia. Yale has approximately 50,000, and the University of Pennsylvania has over 40,000, including 10,000 from the city of Ur, alone. As you'd expect, the translations of the oldest of these Sumerian tablets tell us a great deal about the civilization in which Abraham, his family, and his ancestors had lived and worked. So what *do* we find in these tablets?

They deal with the records that people keep of their lives: records of dowries, marriages, adoptions, divorces, wills, and of course, many commercial transactions. A large percentage of all the tablets translated so far deal in some way with commerce, but even those are interesting.[21]

There are checks, letters of credit, bills of exchange, lists of possessions, loans and records of deposits, limited partnerships, even an early mutual fund. There are also court decrees, lists of professions (ranked socially from high to low), nursing contracts, and apprenticeships. There are even a few free trade agreements between neighboring cities, made in more enlightened times.

Abraham's city of Ur kept written records for its orchestras, choral unions and trade guilds—all sorts of civilized activities. Of course, government transactions were recorded on clay tablets, but even petty government purchases were included. One of the oldest records ever found, written some 5,000 years ago, was a city official's authorization for bread, onions and beer for three messengers going to another city on official business. The team leader of the messengers got twice as much beer as his assistants. That may not have been such a good idea.

Fortunately, some of the tablets are of a more literary nature, and these are of special interest to us. There are many letters, including love letters, and personal diaries. There are also poems, dynastic histories, encyclopedias, and some bilingual and even trilingual dictionaries.

There are expositions on math, law, diagnostic medicine, music, astronomy, prophesy, and so on. Some of these are "book-length," with 10,000 or more lines of writing. The treatise on diagnostic medicine was on 40 large clay tablets.

There are debates, satires, fables, proverbs, and even a few jokes.

One bad joke, apparently by the Sumerian equivalent of Henny Youngman, went like this: *"If you see a poor man drop dead, don't try to revive him! He won't appreciate it."* That has a fair amount of built-in social commentary.

In a dig into the debris pile of Mari, an early satellite city of Ur, French archaeologists found a perfectly preserved, well-cataloged library of 30,000 clay tablets dating as far back as 2700 BCE. Fortunately for our purposes, a great many tablets that deal with temple worship and religion have been found throughout the area.

There are hymns, prayers, lamentations, and a kind of general mythology concerning the deeds of their gods and goddesses. There is also a fair amount about *divine kings,* and that has always been a problem for ordinary citizens.

Until the war in Iraq, several of Sumeria's original cities had not yet been excavated in any way. Iraq had more than 10,000 registered archaeological sites. Keep in mind that we are talking about the ruins of a civilization that flourished 2,000 years before the Greeks.

CHAPTER SIX
Carvers, Writers, Diggers, and a Thinker

Perhaps the most interesting artistic endeavor by the Sumerians was copied by all Mesopotamian successors and, for a time, even by the Egyptians. That was the cylinder seal—the source of most of the images we have of early Sumerian deities. Cylinder seals were recessed negative images carved into stone, ivory, bone, ceramic, and almost any other material that was hard enough to retain the inscribed figures. When a seal was rolled across soft clay, it made a dramatic impression.

Invented some two centuries before the Sumerian language, the cylinder seal was originally a tool for commerce, used to seal the openings of containers, indicate contents, establish identity, and more. Once the Sumerians introduced their written language, they began to seal their letters and documents of all kinds with a cylinder seal clay patch that both identified the sender and testified that the enclosure had not been opened, seen or changed by others.

As religion in Mesopotamia developed to the point of devotional worship, many beautiful cylinder-seal representations of gods and goddesses were made for individuals as a special way to praise and honor their own chosen deity. The carvers of the seals reached very high levels of artistic achievement, even if only in miniature works. Most of the major museums in the United States and Europe have extensive collections of Sumerian (and later) cylinder seals.

Figure 11: Sumerian cylinder seals with their clay imprints

A Sumerian clay tablet that gave us a lamentation and a prayer by a vanquished city king also told how he ridiculed his nomadic conquerors as *"people who don't know flour!"* The implication, of course, was that if you don't eat bread regularly, you must be a barbarian. As agriculture and civilization spread, so did this very notion. Chinese city records, 1,500 or so years later, say much the same thing about the nomads: *"Those people don't know grain!"*

Clay tablets voice two other complaints by the Sumerians against the nomads they knew. For civilized people, these complaints were both valid. The nomads from the Iranian plateau never bathed, and they didn't bury their dead. Perhaps a better distinction between the civilized and uncivilized would have been that, among the nomads, no one could read or write. They left no records of their own experience and, except for woven designs, very little in the way of art.

Whenever we say *"a Sumerian clay tablet tells us,"* we are referring to something written by scribes in cities and towns. It was their job to write, and write they did. From 3300 BCE on, we are in recorded history. By 2700 BCE, the kings were having their decrees written down, not only inscribed on kiln-dried clay tablets, but also cut into stone. That is one way to try for immortality.

So, we have a wonderful record given to us by the scribes and the literate artists in Mesopotamia, from both clay tablets and cylinder seals, and inscriptions on imported stone (floated down from sites well upstream on the Tigris and Euphrates). Their counterparts in Egypt also left behind a fascinating record, first on clay tablets and then on papyrus sealed in jars, on tomb walls written in paint and inscriptions cut into stone, and even in bas-relief presentations.

Figure 12: Sumerian and Egyptian court scribes

From their scribes, we know, for example, that in Sumeria a woman could be a judge, a scribe, an accountant or a priestess; could run a tavern; own, buy and sell property; lend and borrow money; and remarry if she became widowed. Early Sumerian codes protected these rights for women by law.

The Sumerian scribes also left a record of their popular songs—and they were as hackneyed as many of ours. (One

Sumerian song had the opening line: *"I'm crazy with love for you!"*) But the scribes also inserted a note of reality. In their earliest myths, the goddess of love was the sister of her greatest enemy, the goddess of death.

Scribes were assigned the task of writing down everything that happened—in trade, in military campaigns, in agricultural production, and more. They took inventories, but also recorded the religious life of the day in myths, hymns and prayers. Because of their particular combination of literacy, intelligence, and presence, scribes often held official positions in the bureaucracy of ancient cities, particularly in the second and third tiers of city administration.

They had the original "white collar" jobs, without the white collars. Scribes had a keen awareness that they lived a privileged life, and often commented on just that in letters to their children. No other occupation held such promise or offered such consistent rewards for a lay member of society. Will Durant commented on the *princely dignity* of the scribe, adding that *"...he had just enough intelligence not to be dangerous."*[22]

But there were such things as lazy scribes, as you might guess. One letter from an Egyptian minister to a scribe who held an official position included this stern warning: *"You will not slack on this job! I know you are sluggish!"*[23] An archaeologist found that letter 3,100 years later still unopened. In spite of the occasional lazy scribe, they served their masters well. We are forever in their debt.

The world may well one day have a full account of Mesopotamian civilization, thanks to that part of the world's dry climate, the blowing sands, and those ancient scribes. Indeed, we are still involved in the process of discovery. In Iraq alone, there could easily be another million clay tablets buried in those 10,000 recognized archaeological sites that dot the landscape. However, with the ravages brought by the Iraq war, continuing political conflict, damage to archaeological sites, and a lack of trained scholars, it may be that we will never know this civilization fully. The process of discovery will be an interesting one, however.

It is easy for us to forget that until a little over 200 years ago, no one knew that the Sumerians had ever existed. We couldn't understand any of their language until about 150 years ago, and we didn't really determine that their language was truly an *isolate*—that it had no known ties to any other language—until the last 50 years or so.

We should also take a moment to acknowledge the early archaeologists, many of whom were simply *interested amateurs*. Unfortunately, many of their methods were so crude that they destroyed about as much of the past as they preserved.

Henry Layard is an example of an untrained archaeologist at work. He was a wealthy young Englishman who decided to travel on horseback from Europe to India, accompanied by a friend. On his way, he visited Petra, in what is now Jordan, and Layard was fascinated. When he got to those ancient mounds in northern Iraq, he hired crews and just tunneled in.

Luck seemed to be Layard's middle name. In 1845, in one of those mounds, Layard discovered the ruins of Kalhu (biblical Calah), one of the old capital cities of Assyria. He sent whole shiploads of statuary, bas-relief, and wall paintings—anything large and spectacular—to establish his name back in Great Britain. Another Englishman, Howard Carter, more professional than Layard, found King Tut's tomb in Egypt in 1922, and achieved instant fame.

Leonard Wooley was a British spy who learned Arabic while locked up in a Turkish prison. Wooley stayed on in the Middle East to excavate Ur in southern Iraq from 1922 to 1934. Fortunately he was assisted by professional archaeologists from the University of Pennsylvania. The majority of Woolley's findings—particularly the large and colorful ones—went to British museums. However, he shared many of the finest smaller pieces with the University of Pennsylvania, which has a superb Museum of Archaeology and Anthropology in Philadelphia. With choice artifacts from Ur and Nippur, it is well worth a visit.

The University of Pennsylvania and the University of Chicago did a joint dig in Nippur just after World War II. If you went to the Beijing Olympics, you may have seen a number of the best items from the University of Pennsylvania's collection on display. China had borrowed them to help attract a crowd!

We are fortunate that the cover of sand and the dry climate saved as much of the record of this ancient civilization as it did. Of course, from the beginning, a major problem was that no one could read the writing. Sumerian was an undeciphered language even though several linguists had tried to decipher it.

The first true breakthrough came in the early 1800s, when the British East India Company sent a bright young officer, Henry Rawlinson, on loan from India to Persia (now Iran), to help reorganize the Shah's army. At Behistan, at the foot of the Zagros Mountains in Persia, Rawlinson was fascinated by a great inscription in three unknown languages, carved side by side into the face of a large cliff, all in cuneiform writing.

With the help of one young assistant, Rawlinson lowered himself on ropes onto the face of the cliff. He made clay-imprint copies of the one language that looked most promising for translation. Rawlinson guessed correctly—the one he chose turned out to be a cuneiform version of Old Persian. Old Persian also had an alphabetic form that closely resembled Sanskrit, the ancient and sacred language of the Aryans who settled in India. Rawlinson was already fluent in Sanskrit.

A Persian scholar helped him work out the transition from cuneiform to alphabetic writing for Old Persian, and Rawlinson took it from there, in Sanskrit. Rawlinson made the assumption that in a trilingual inscription like the one on the great cliff, all three of the languages—whatever they may be—were all saying the same thing. He was right.

Fortunately for us, one of the other two languages on the cliff face was the old language *Akkadian*, belonging to the first conquerors of Sumeria. Akkadian was also undeciphered at that time. Over the course of 12 years of hard work, Rawlinson was able to work from Old Persian to Sanskrit to Akkadian, and he thoroughly deciphered Akkadian. There was some bad news and some good news.

The bad news was that the third language on the face of the cliff was not Sumerian. It was a little-known language now known as New Elamite. It is still largely indecipherable in spite of its prevalence in the early part of the Persian Empire. Elam references the area around the old city of Susa (Sushan), and both are commonly referenced in the Old Testament.[24]

The really good news was that among the many cuneiform clay tablets dug up in Mesopotamia were bilingual dictionaries of Akkadian and Sumerian. That also made it possible to decipher the Sumerian language—the language of the first true civilization.

CHAPTER SEVEN
Deities, Kings, and Temples

When Abraham (as Abram) lived in the city of Ur, the Sumerian city system along the southern reaches of the Tigris-Euphrates had been in existence for at least 1,500 years, and parts of it for more than 3,000 years. Religion played a major role in the lives of those who lived in this first civilization, as it had for those who lived in earlier times. The record of Mesopotamian mythology begins with the advent of writing, but it tells of much that had developed long before.

The civilization that was first recorded by the Sumerians was absorbed, revised, or otherwise continued by the Akkadians, the Babylonians, and so on, until its final destruction. Widespread recording in the Sumerian language ended by about 2,000 BCE. From then on, dialects of the Semitic language, Akkadian, were dominant.

Loan words from Sumerian were commonplace in Akkadian and, vice versa, leading to a strong "linguistic convergence." However, Sumerian would eventually become the formal classical language for Mesopotamia, with special uses, and was often the choice for literary works. Latin would be a reasonable parallel of that, many centuries later.

Sumerian mythological themes continued on also in Akkadian, with whatever revisions of name and authority that new rulers and new priests deemed fit. The last Akkadian writing in cuneiform dates to about 75 CE, but another Semitic language, Aramaic, had displaced it in popular speech from about 700 BCE. Part of the widespread appeal of Aramaic was that it was alphabetic, and thus easier to learn.

Scholars do not agree as to when the end came for this Sumerian-based Mesopotamian civilization. Most British and American archaeologists concluded that it ended with the Persian conquest in 539 BCE. One French scholar, Jean Boterro, decided that it ended some 250 years later, after an invasion by the Parthians from the Iranian plateau. Perhaps we should settle for the fact that from the time of its conquest by the Persians under Cyrus the Great, the Mesopotamian area which followed Sumerian culture was never again ruled by anyone born there. Greek and Roman conquerors would soon be on the scene.

A common observation in the literature is that Sumeria was a *polytheistic* society. That is more than a mild understatement. The Sumerians, and all those who borrowed and built on their culture, were up to their eyebrows in anthropomorphic gods and goddesses, who had divine children who had divine children, and so on. Every aspect of life, material or otherwise, had a mythical being assigned to it. Most individuals wisely settled for devotion to one deity, and not necessarily the god or goddess that was adopted by the city where they lived.

Over this enormous time frame of 3,000 years, gods and goddesses changed their names, their form, their function, and occasionally their gender. Divine lineages were reinvented, suggesting completely new sets of parents and progeny. Many deities disappeared, while some had reincarnations. Archaeologists and linguists have counted several thousand names for divinities over the course of some 2,800 years of writing in Mesopotamian cultural areas. We will look at only a few who are prominent in the stories that most interest us, laying a foundation for the ideas and the stories in the Old Testament.

With successive invasions by groups having nomadic, patriarchal backgrounds, goddesses often lost out to male gods. However, one goddess persisted, even with some name and function changes. She was *INANNA*, the Sumerian Queen of Heaven. Old clay tablets refer to Inanna as the Virgin Mother, but at least one worthy scholarly work states rather emphatically that she was neither a mother goddess nor a goddess of marriage.[25]

Well, Inanna was seldom depicted as overweight or pregnant, so perhaps that helped persuade the authors to avoid the Mother Goddess label. It may have been because Inanna was the goddess of sexual love. Inanna meets that description fully, particularly in Akkadian-Babylonian form as *ISHTAR*, but in the early Sumerian mythology, Inanna was worshipped and depicted as a warrior as well as a goddess of fertility and love.

Figure 13: Sumerian king led by a lesser goddess to worship Inanna, Queen of Heaven

Inanna deserves special mention because the first formal literary works, as such, were hymns to her. Inanna's primary city was Uruk, where there were women priestesses and women serving along with men as judges. Inanna's temple at Uruk is believed to have been functioning as early as 4,000 BCE. Although the spiritual leader (en) of her temple was a male, there were no other priests, only priestesses.

The scribes who kept the Queen of Heaven's accounts were all women. There is a strong probability that these female scribes invented the first written language as something needed beyond the keeping of financial records. Along with the priestesses, they had the best opportunity to move from the temple's commercial accounts to a more expressive worship of Inanna through recorded hymns of praise.

In Sumeria's intertwined cosmology and theology, Inanna represented the planet we know as Venus. She was hailed as both the Morning Star and the Evening Star. One of the oldest cylinder seals attests to this view, as does the inconstant mythology that developed around Inanna. She could be active on earth, then disappear to battle death in the grim Sumerian underworld, come back again into another earthly drama, and participate in the resurrection of her lover.

Among the male gods, *ENLIL* was widely worshipped as the God of the Wind and Air. (In Akkadian and other languages in the Mesopotamian culture area, Enlil became Ellil.) Just as Inanna was the principal goddess in Mesopotamian mythology, Enlil was the principal god, the Ruler of All the Lands. His dominance stemmed from power inherited from divine parents, from his role in an early creation myth, from his popular recognition as the founder of agriculture, and as the god who controls the future of the Universe—the holder of the Tablet of Destinies.[26]

Enlil's patron city was Nippur, which in accordance with his stature, was Sumeria's holiest city. In the first of the two main Sumerian versions of creation that were borrowed and only slightly revised for Genesis, Enlil separated a joined heaven and earth, and then kept heaven for him to rule.[27]

ENKI was the Sumerian god of fresh water and god of wisdom. His city was Eridu, Sumeria's oldest, and for that good reason, Enki is credited with founding civilization. In the Akkadian mythology that followed the Sumerians, Enki's counterpart was the god *EA*. Possibly because irrigation water and trade by water were so beneficial to them, Ea's followers believed that Ea loved people.

Sun gods also played important roles in Mesopotamian religious culture. *UTU* was the Sumerian sun god; his Akkadian name was *SHAMASH*. It makes sense that, over time, Utu also became the God of Justice, because in the bright light of the sun, no secrets could be hidden. Utu's stature in the pantheon of deities is reinforced by his being the twin brother of Inanna, Goddess of Heaven and Earth. In one of several different myths suggesting their lineage, Utu's and Inanna's parents were *NANNA* (the moon god) and *NINGAL* (the Great Lady, Goddess of the Reeds.)[28]

In a combination prayer-lament, Sin-iddiam, King of the city of Larsa, addressed Utu through his scribe:

> *"Say to Utu, my lord, the exalted judge of heaven and earth, who renders verdicts as a just god, who loves to keep man alive, who heeds entreaty, who extends mercy, who knows compassion, who loves justice, who selects honesty, who is the father of the black-headed people..."*[29]

Justice, mercy, and compassion were among the attributes of the best of these early divine beings, and the Sumerians wrote about them in praise long before anything had been written about the god of the Old Testament.

Near the Sumerian city of Lagash was the temple for the goddess *NANSHE*. In Sumerian mythology, Nanshe was the daughter of ENKI, the god of water. She was a goddess with an interesting set of responsibilities including fishing, prophesy, and social justice. But from her special role with social justice, Nanshe evolved into a goddess who deserved to be worshipped by everyone. Here are a few excerpts adapted from a long hymn of praise for Nanshe, found on a clay tablet in the ruins of Lagash:

> *"It is She who knows the orphan and aids the widow; it is She who seeks justice for the poor,*

and shelters the weak. It is She who provides for refugees. She does not forget those who help others. May Nanshe be praised in all the countries."[30]

Each Sumerian city had its own special deity. In Ur, where Abraham's family lived, the moon god Nanna was the deity to which that city was dedicated. Nanna was a male divinity, although in Mesopotamia's long and complex mythology, there were moon goddesses as well.

Just as the temple of the goddess Inanna in the city of Uruk chose a man as their spiritual leader *(en)*, the *en* for the temple of the god Nanna at Ur was a woman, the high-priestess of the Temple of Inanna.

Gods and goddesses lived in a skyward heaven, but it was reserved for them. No humans could aspire to reach it. However, gods and goddesses also resided in the temples that humans built for them, and that gave a human worshipper a chance to form a closer relationship. By the time writing was commonplace in Sumerian history, from about 2700 BCE onward, you were free to choose your own personal god.

Devotion would include offerings given to the temple priests of that god or goddess. Due to the small size of most temples, it is likely that most personal prayers were made at home. However, one could give the temple priest small figurines made specifically to *say prayers continuously* on your behalf.

Figure 14: Small votive sculptures

The monumental temple-tower that some Sumerian cities built for their own chosen deity was the *ziggurat*, but it was inaccessible to the ordinary citizen once it was built. There was no space provided for a congregation of worshippers.

A ziggurat began as a gigantic stack of sun-dried brick, confined by colorfully painted walls of fired brick. Some of the earliest ziggurats had only two or three levels but, over time, a seven-storied ziggurat declared the extent of a city's devotion to its chosen deity. On top of the last terrace was a small temple dedicated to the god or goddess of the city, a holy of holies entered only by the priests.

The Ur ziggurat was built by the Sumerian king Ur-Nammu, in the 21st century BCE. As reconstructed below, it had three terraced levels and, on top of those, a temple reaching toward the sky.

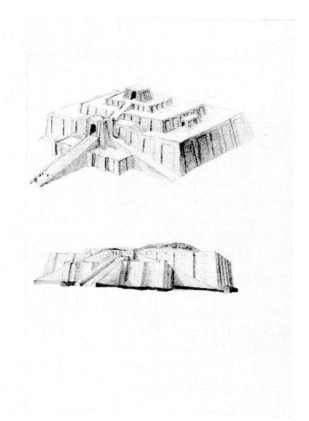

Figure 15: The ziggurat at UR
Upper: Artist's conception of the ziggurat in its prime
Lower: The lower-level façade as reconstructed by
Saddam Hussein

Around 550 BCE, the last of the neo-Babylonian kings, Nabonidus, rebuilt the disintegrated Ur ziggurat, but elevated it to seven levels. The British archaeologist, Sir Leonard Wooley, found enough information to have an architectural drawing made of Ur's last ziggurat.

**Figure 16: Drawing of Nabonidus'
reconstruction of the ziggurat at Ur**

The original ziggurat at Ur had a massive first level as the main platform, then two successively smaller levels on top of the base. That large first layer was 200 feet long, 140 feet wide, and 70 feet high. The first layer was painted white, the second layer was painted black, and the third layer was painted red. At the top was a temple dedicated to Ur's chosen deity, Nanna, the moon god. The top of the temple was about 200 feet above ground level. On a clear day, Ur's ziggurat was visible from about 20 miles away across the flat countryside.

Sumerians knew that important things came from the mountains—their water, their lumber and stone, precious metals and jewels, and even the pitch that sealed their boats. Surely the gods and goddesses would want to have an earthly dwelling place on a mountain, even if it were man-made. *"Our god is on high!"* Or, *"Our goddess is in a high place!"* The temple on top of any ziggurat was meant to be the place where heaven and earth came together. But down on the ground were the ordinary political issues of life.

For the first 500 years or so, Sumerian cities were ruled by councils of elders. However, in times of danger, the council would appoint a military leader, the Lugal. Lugal meant *The Big Man.* Eventually there was one big man too many, and the Lugal declared himself to be the king. The most ancient Sumerian king for which there is a representation is shown wearing a military helmet. After that one, all king head-dresses represent their royalty and, all too soon, their role as representative of the gods.

Besides the ego trip, this last move was most likely a tactic by the king to counter the power of the priests. The largest temple complex of a thriving city often became enormously wealthy. The wealth came in part from gifts from the faithful, in part from controlling a large portion of the city's trade, and through ownership of much of the agricultural land around that city.

The king of each city relied on taxes and tribute. Because the king normally appointed military leaders and provided their funding, the king would squeeze the priesthood and the citizenry for extra support if he felt the city needed a new wall, some updated arms, or a military campaign against a troublesome neighbor..

Only one woman, Kug-Bao, was ever listed in the Sumerian king list. She ruled in about 25th Century BCE. The reason for the approximation is that Kug-Bao is recorded in the king's list as having held power for 100 years. She is identified as Queen of the city of Kish, and cited as *"Kug-Bao, the woman tavern-keeper who made firm the foundations of Kish,"* by casting off the rule of the city of Lagash.[31]

CHAPTER EIGHT
Laments, Prayer, and Hymns

The Bible does not tell us when Abraham's Semitic ancestors moved to Ur, where the moon god, Nanna, was the official city deity. Sumeria was first conquered by a warrior-leader named Sargon I, whose Semitic tribesmen overran Sumeria around 2330 BCE. Abraham's family may have arrived shortly after Sargon's conquest. They later identified the city of Haran, in southeastern Anatolia (now Turkey), as their home area. It is interesting to note that Haran also had the Sumerian moon god, Nanna, as its primary deity. Perhaps that made their move more comfortable.

No one knows how long Abraham's family lived in Ur, but most certainly long enough to absorb much of the culture. If they came shortly after Sargon I captured Ur, a good guess would be about 325 years, but some scholarly estimates have been as high as four centuries.

Most biblical scholars believe that Abraham's immediate family members were animal traders. A city such as Ur required thousands of sheep and goats annually for meat. Ur's own agricultural hinterland couldn't provide nearly enough, as it was largely under cultivation. Records on a clay tablet from one Sumerian city, smaller than Ur, recorded that in one year it had consumed 30,000 sheep and 120,000 goats. Supplying meat for any city was a big business.

As urban meat providers, members of Abraham's family would cross over the desert to the highlands, where nomads herded animals. There they would trade products manufactured in the city, such as cloth, jewelry, and perhaps clandestinely, metal weapons—and then bring animals back to sell in Ur, the dominant city in Mesopotamia at the time.

At its largest, Ur probably had about 40,000 people living inside the city walls. Thousands of others lived just outside the walls and worked in or for the city of Ur. Size did not determine importance, necessarily. In terms of population and area, the city of Uruk was perhaps twice as large as Ur, but not as dominant, either culturally or politically.

Things could go badly wrong for any city. Floods or sudden changes in the course of the river on which the city was dependent for water and trade could mean difficult times. Warfare with neighboring city-states was bad enough, but invasion by uncivilized nomadic warriors was the worst fear. Huge numbers came down from the plateau and highlands to the east on foot, with their provisions, shields, and heavy weapons in ox carts. Their aims were total destruction and easy looting afterward.

A gripping lamentation could be written by a literate observer, or it might be the king in the last stages of losing his position, his power, and his people. (In many cases, the king was a part of the spoils taken away by the conquering army.)

Lamentations might turn to those improbable conquerors, deploring the cultural failings of the invading enemy—barbarians who came from places without roads, who did not eat bread because they did not grow grain, who never bathed, and did not even bury their dead. How, they ask, could their great city have been overwhelmed by such as these?

The accounts of the agony of those facing destruction within the city are harrowing. There were crises of faith: The lamenter might question or condemn the god or goddess of the city who failed to give it protection; would mention disdainfully other deities with local temples who also did not come to the city's aid; and would again bemoan the destruction and sad fate of the city.

Hymns of praise were usually directed at the god or goddess chosen as a personal deity to act as intercessor with all the other divine beings who might affect the course of your life. Here is a small part of a hymn to Enlil, the Sumerian god of the air:

"Without Enlil, the great mountain,
No cities would be built, no settlements founded.
No stalls would be built, no sheepfold erected.
No king enthroned, no high priest born. —
In field and meadow, the rich grain would fail to flower.
Without Him, the trees planted on the mountain
Would not even yield their fruit."[32]

Reading a few literary pieces from Sumerian and Babylonian times gives us a sense of what was happening in personal worship 40 centuries ago. The first piece, "*To Inanna*," was written by Enheduanna, the well-educated daughter of Sargon I, conqueror of Sumer, and founder of the first Akkadian empire.

In a wise political move, Sargon sent Enheduanna to be the spiritual leader, in this case *en priestess*, for the temple dedicated to Ur's moon god, Nanna. In doing that, he set a trend. For the next 500 years, Mesopotamian rulers sent daughters, sisters, and nieces as *en priestesses* to Nanna's temple in Ur.

Although Enheduanna served that temple well, she was considerably more interested in worshipping the goddess Inanna, whom she had chosen as her personal deity. When writing hymns and poems dedicated to Inanna, Enheduanna made it clear that she had written them, becoming the first person in human history to be identified as the author of any literary work.

The hymn *"To Inanna"* was one of Enheduanna's moon-lighting hymns to the Sumerian Queen of Heaven and Earth. In it, Enheduanna refers twice to the *mes* or the *life-giving divine decrees*. This is a reference to a particular piece of Sumerian mythology that says that Inanna's father was Enki (Ea), the god of water and wisdom. He was the ruling god of the first city, Eridu. Enki had created Eridu out of his divine decrees, each of which, in Sumerian, was called a *"me."* The *mes*, then, describe the attributes of a city. They are all the things found, *good and bad*, in a complex metropolis. One of Enki's functions was to protect these divine decrees.

According to myth, Inanna wanted to restore the great-ness of her own city, Uruk, and needed her own set of divine decrees. At first, Enki is unwilling to part with them. With the help of 14 successive drinks, Inanna out-foxes her father and makes off with many of his sacred *mes.* (He gave her a few after each drink.) After a perilous flight, Inanna uses the sto-len divine decrees to enrich Uruk, the world's second oldest city. Uruk became the main center of Inanna worship. These are some of the *mes* Inanna brought to Uruk:

"Truth, art, music, goodness, justice, writing, carpentry, metalwork, leather-work, masonry, basket-weaving, wisdom, understanding, fear, fire, weariness, strife, peace, victory, defeat, shouting, counsel, judgment, decision,

exuberance, legal speech, illegal speech, sexual intercourse, prostitution, oral sex, straightforwardness, enmity, descent to and ascent from the underworld, kingship with crown and throne, destruction of cities, rebellion, sorrow, and rejoicing."[33]

It makes one wonder whether there has ever been a civilization quite as self-conscious as that of Sumeria. Here is a small part of *"To Inanna,"* one of Enheduanna's many hymns:[34]

"TO INANNA
Queen, greater than An, King of Heaven,
Who has paid you homage!
You, who in accordance with
The life-giving divine decrees,
Great queen of queens, ...
Merciful, life-giving woman, radiant of heart!"

A rather different poetic approach is shown in this excerpt of a beautiful hymn to Inanna called *"The Lady of the Morning:"*[35]

"Honored Counselor, Ornament of Heaven, Joy of An!
When sweet sleep has ended in the bedchamber,

You appear like bright daylight. ...
My Lady looks in sweet wonder from heaven.
The people of Sumer parade before the holy Inanna.
Inanna, the Lady of the Morning, is radiant."

The next poem is written as though it were advice from a father to his son. Remember, the Akkadian-Babylonians who succeeded the Sumerians in Mesopotamia, were male-oriented and patriarchal. Their literature is often speaking to the men. Men were admonished to worship God every day, give offerings, pray and ask forgiveness for their sins. A main theme was *stay in harmony with God.*

> *"Let your mouth be restrained, and your speech guarded*
> *That is a man's pride—let what you say be very precious.*
> *Let insolence and blasphemy be an abomination for you.*
> *A talebearer is looked down upon...*
> *Do not return evil to your adversary;*
> *Requite with kindness the one who does evil to you;*
> *Maintain justice for your enemy;*
> *Be friendly to your enemy...*
> *Give him food to eat, beer to drink;*
> *Grant what is requested;*

Provide for him, and treat him with honor.
At this your God takes pleasure...
Do good things; be kind all your days."[36]

For anyone with a Judeo-Christian background, this is an interesting poem. *Proverbs* 25:21 will borrow an important thought from the poem: *"If your enemy is hungry, give him food to eat; if he is thirsty, give him water to drink."* (You probably noticed that the Hebrew writers cut the beer.) The god addressed in the poem was the Babylonian sun god, *Shamash.*

The last poem, *"A Babylonian Penitential Prayer,"* was written after the competition between gods and goddesses was well underway. It is an interesting and sensible solution to that particular gender issue when making a personal appeal in those times. This prayer was found on a clay tablet written in Sumerian, but composed in Babylonian times.

"I, your servant, full of sighs, cry unto you.
Accept the fervent prayer of one burdened with sin.
Whoever you look upon, lives!
Look with true favor on me, and accept my supplication.
How long, my God?
How long, my Goddess, until your face is turned to me?
How long, known and unknown God, until the anger
   of your heart is appeased?

How long, known and unknown Goddess, until your
  unfriendly heart is appeased?
(Mankind is perverted, and has no judgment;
Of all who are alive, who really knows anything?
They do not know whether they do good or evil!)
O Lord, do not cast aside your servant;
I am cast into the mire: take my hand!
The sin which I have sinned, turn to mercy!
The iniquity which I have committed let the wind carry
  away.
Tear off my many transgressions like a garment!
My God, my sins are seven times seven; forgive my
  sins!
My Goddess, my sins are seven times seven; forgive
  my sins!
Forgive my sins, and I will humble myself before you.
May your heart, as the heart of a mother
Who has borne children, be glad;
As a mother who has borne children,
As a father who has begotten, may it be glad![37]

It is helpful to consider the ways in which people received messages from the gods and goddesses. It could be from deities speaking directly to someone—usually to kings or high priests, who were, perhaps, the ancient equivalent of our politicians and televangelists. However, *"God said to me"* was not a very common phrase in Mesopotamian culture areas. More usual were visions in which *"God made known to me"* something of importance.

Much more involved in the life of the people were the dreams that anyone could have whenever they slept. This was the common person's glimpse into the mysteries of the divine: *What the gods and goddesses had decided would happen to me!* You saw dreams: they were the *products of the night.*

As you would expect, translating dreams became a very good business, as it still is today. At one archaeological site, tablets were found with some 4,000 interpretations of dreams. And in that particular dig, only a little over half the anticipated number of tablets were found.

Certainly, dreams and visions are common themes in the Old Testament. Dream interpretation is a major item for both Joseph and Daniel. Some of the Old Testament prophets got pretty indignant about common people thinking their own dreams were meaningful, so both Jeremiah and Zechariah have really harsh things to say about *empty dreamers.*

In the book of Job, dreams are said first to be authentic means of divine communication, and then later, said to be fleeting and insubstantial. But the Sumerian practices and beliefs regarding dreams seem to have set the pattern not only for almost all the Middle East, including early Judaism, but also for Greece in a later time.

Prayer was a means of getting messages to the gods and goddesses. As we've already mentioned, prayer played a major role in the lives of ordinary citizens of Mesopotamia. And among kings, it was common custom to have their prayers written down by scribes.

As with public prayer today, generally you could foretell the strength of a prayer by its opening lines. One that I noticed from Sumeria was addressed to Nanna, the moon god of Ur. It began: *"Merciful father, in whose hands the life of the whole land lies..."* Not so long ago, PBS replayed a superb video of Marian Anderson singing, *"He's got the whole world, in his hands"*—and I thought of those lines written in Ur more than 4,000 years before.

CHAPTER NINE
Laws and Lawmakers

We all owe a special debt to the Sumerians, who in the earliest civilization repeatedly appealed for justice under the law. This is true, even if their law seems harsh to us. The Sumerian scribes wrote: *Justice is the arrow that keeps society on a straight path.*

A relevant and compelling story comes to us from the city of Lagash. It is such an interesting tale that I once wrote it up as a scenario for a thoughtful group that dramatized historical events. Here is the general outline of that story, as I presented it.

Near the year 2380 BCE, the King of Lagash died, but there was no suitable heir to replace him. City elders selected a young nobleman to be their new king.[38] His name was *Urukagina*, a name we ought to know and honor.

Soon after Urukagina was installed as king of Lagash, he began a major reform campaign, possibly the first in recorded history. He called in the chief scribe to prepare a royal edict.

There were six major orders in the edict, and Urukagina explained to the scribe why he was ordering such radical changes in the life of the city. The scribe's jaw must have dropped a few inches. The scribe recorded this dramatic event and even recorded his own participation in the exchange. Urukagina said:

"1. *From this day forward, no priest can collect taxes! Those stupid people are not just overtaxing, they are taking away what the people have to have in order to pay taxes next year—the fisherman's boat, the farmer's ox, the weaver's loom. Those wretched priests are even stealing the bread that people provide their dead loved ones so they can have a decent start in the Netherworld!*

2. *From this day forward, no member of the royal family may hold a senior post in the city's administration! Those greedy parasites are living on bribes!*

3. *From this day forward, any person of wealth mistreating a poor person will be punished! Landlords are taking the fruit off the trees of poor widows!*

4. *From this day forward, any merchant found cheating a poor person will be punished! This is happening everywhere, and it will be stopped!*

5. *From this day forward, all persons imprisoned for debt are to be released from prison. How can a city possibly benefit by keeping its citizens from working?*

6. *From this day forward, all persons enslaved for debt are to be released from slavery. We need other solutions."*

The scribe: *"Would you like to say given 'freedom?' That is a word some of the scribes are using."*
Urukagina: *"How do you write 'freedom?'"*
Scribe: *"Either Amargi —'return to mother', or 'broken chains.'"*
Urukagina: *"In my city, there shall be freedom!"*

Although archaeologists have not yet found a copy of his edict establishing a code of laws, Urukagina did develop a legal guide. Many of his rulings have been discovered in other contexts, including one that made polyandry illegal, and one that exempted widows and orphans from paying taxes.

Almost certainly, he built his own law code on others already existing. The very first city, Eridu, must have had a law code in some form in 5100 BCE. It would be impossible for any city to operate effectively without certain known standards of legal behavior. More law codes followed and were compiled by later kings.

Some two centuries after Urukagina, in 2141 BCE, another memorable king came to the throne in Lagash. His name was Gudea, and we know his face because more statues of Gudea have been found than of any other Sumerian king—27 to be exact.[39] At first, archaeologists assumed that most of these were simply copies of older originals, but on closer examination, every one of them proved to be an original.

Figure 17: King Gudea of Lagash

Gudea's image was in demand, partly because he ordered the first modest one to commemorate his rule, and partly because there were few rulers like Gudea. Clay tablets and stone inscriptions credit him for purifying the city, morally and ethically. Included in Gudea's instructions to the people of Lagash was an admonition that they should never, ever beat their children. Another was that children should never speak harshly to their mothers. Slave owners should never strike a slave, even if the slave had shown disrespect, and so on.

Numerous clay tablets cite Gudea for building and supporting a large number of temples dedicated to both goddesses and gods. However, the temples in return were expected to assume social responsibilities to help those in need in the city: the impoverished, the ill and the isolated. One of Gudea's main accomplishments was to revise and update Urukagina's law code for the city of Lagash.

Like Urukagina, Gudea was personally concerned about the welfare of the poor. One surviving tablet suggests that the city's more privileged classes assassinated Gudea after only a seven-year reign. At any rate, a highly unusual event occurred after his death: The common people threatened to rebel unless King Gudea was declared to have been divine— to have been a god.

Perhaps this was one of the few ways the lower classes had of reminding the royal families how kings should behave. Unfortunately, there were plenty of lesser kings that wanted to be declared divine while they were alive and ruling, and that meant trouble for the ordinary citizen.

Gudea must have been a hard act to follow. Here is an excerpt from a clay tablet inscription found in the ruins of Lagash:

> *"During the seven years of King Gudea's reign, the maidservant was the equal of her mistress; the slave worked beside his master, and in this city, the weak rested by the side of the strong!"*

The ideal of fairness is every bit as old as that of justice under the law. One of the first fully recorded court cases in human history deals with both those issues. The tablets that tell about it are from early Babylonian times. The case involves a murder charge brought against the wife of a man who baked for a temple. The wife hired three men to kill her husband by a nearby river on his way home from work. They were not too secretive about it, and nine people saw the men beat the baker to death. When the men were arrested, they placed the blame on the wife who hired them.

At the trial, the nine witnesses for the prosecution testified first. Near the end of the trial, the wife brought in two neighbors as the only witnesses for her defense. Both neighbors testified that she was beaten almost every day by her husband. The court let her go free, but executed the killers and buried them just in front of the door of her home. Then the court ordered that her husband be buried under the floor of her home.

Four thousand years later, here in Austin, there was a similar case in which a severely abused wife hired two men to kill her husband by the Colorado River. When the men were arrested, they placed the blame on the wife who hired them. The Babylonian judgments were certainly more imaginative than those in the Austin case. In Austin, the wife and the assailants were all given prison sentences.

In 2113 BCE, after throwing off the rule of the Akkadians, the city of Ur began its final and finest period of cultural revival and creativity. The first king of this dynamic, century-long era was one of the greatest, a Sumerian named Ur-Nammu. Ur-Nammu is credited with formulating a major law code based largely on Gudea's updating of Urukagina's law code.

It is interesting that, in general, Ur-Nammu's law code of 2113 BCE is not nearly as severe as most of the later law codes. That includes Hammurabi's law code created in 1730 BCE and laws credited to Moses around 1200 BCE that are found in the Old Testament books of *Leviticus* and *Numbers*. (Those harsh laws are not the Ten Commandments, which are found in *Exodus* and *Deuteronomy*.)

In Ur, under Ur-Nammu, even crimes involving physical injury and death were not automatically subject to retaliatory death or mutilation, as the laws of both Hammurabi and Moses would often require. In Ur, such crimes were sometimes punished by imprisonment or fines collected in silver. Civil offenses in Ur were nearly all punished by fines. For example, the fine for perjury was 15 shekels of silver. A shekel was about half an ounce and considered a heavy fine.

Hammurabi was a great Babylonian king who came to power about 1750 BCE, or more than 350 years after the Sumerian king Ur-Nammu. There are still textbooks that refer to Hammurabi as the author of the first law code, but that isn't true. He had only revised Ur-Nammu's law code, and not all for the better.

The most nearly complete version of Hammurabi's law code was found in the ruins of Susa (biblical *Sushan*) on the Iranian plateau. It had been inscribed on a stone stele—an engraved rock—then looted by the Elamites from a Babylonian city on a raid into Mesopotamia.

Figure 18: Hammurabi

**Figure 19: Hammurabi receiving the
law codes from the Babylonian sun god Shamash,
who is seated on his throne.**

In the preface to his law code, Hammurabi gives a little credit to the gods and a lot to himself, justifiably. He says that he was called by the gods to cause justice to prevail in the land, to destroy the wicked and evil, to prevent the strong from oppressing the weak, to enlighten the land, and to further the welfare of the people. Then he lists his laws and ends with a general repeat of the preface, praising the gods a little and himself a great deal.

His law code ended at law number 282. Actually, there were only 281 laws, because there was no number 13. Even back in 1730 BCE, the Babylonians believed that 13 was a very unlucky number. Hammurabi's laws were generally organized around specific topics or themes such as commerce, real estate, personal property, labor, injury and liability, and family law.

Law No. 23 declared that if you were robbed anywhere in Hammurabi's empire and the local authorities could not capture the thief or thieves and return your property, then you were to go to your local temple. In the presence of the priests or priestesses, and by implication in the presence of the god or goddess of the temple, you gave an itemized account of all that had been stolen. The temple scribe wrote down your statement. The city and the governor of the district where the robbery occurred were then required to compensate you fully for your losses. Hammurabi didn't quite separate church and state, but he did create an interesting system of compensation for losses. It put great pressure on local officials to make their domains safe for travelers.

As did Urukagina and Gudea many centuries earlier, Hammurabi knew that *fairness* was at the heart of righteous behavior. In Law 148 he said:

> *"If a man take a wife, and she be seized by disease, if he then desire to take a second wife he shall not put away his wife, who has been*

attacked by disease, but he shall keep her in the house which he has built and support her so long as she lives."

One notable edict by Hammurabi, given outside his law code, concerned litigation in Babylonia. No civil case could go to court until a serious effort had been made to settle out of court through mediation. We could still benefit from following Hammurabi's code on this point some 3,700 years later.

What we would not want to follow were these early societies' punishments, which outside of the cities of Ur and Lagash were often extremely harsh. Punishments were often pushed toward *equivalent retaliation*—an eye for an eye, a tooth for a tooth—to fit the case. Some cases called for throwing the guilty party into the river, and in some cases, throwing the accused party into the nearest river in order to determine guilt or innocence. If you didn't drown, you weren't guilty!

A mere *accusation* that you were a sorcerer or a witch would get you thrown into the river automatically—no proof required. However, if you survived being thrown into the river, you got all the property of the accuser. That *trial by water* method might encourage a lot of folks to take swimming lessons and perhaps even crocodile wrestling, if that was available.

Any number of scholars and reference texts suggest that Moses borrowed the seven secular commandments in the Ten Commandments from Hammurabi's code. In a very real way, that is misleading. Remember that the first three commandments relate to God: no other gods before me, make no graven images, and do not take God's name in vain. Then come the seven secular ones accredited to Hammurabi. There are two about your home life—resting on the seventh day, and honoring your father and mother. Then come the five no-no's: no murder, adultery, stealing, lying, or coveting. The truth is that all seven of these secular ideas had been promoted in Sumeria more than 1,500 years before Hammurabi, and Hammurabi lived 500 years before Moses.

We should note, however, that in 2010, archaeologists working in a park in Israel found fragments of two clay tablets containing legal pronouncements written in the Akkadian language. They date back some 3,700 years to the time of Hammurabi. As with Hammurabi, the judgments or penalties reflect the idea of *equivalent retaliation*. Clearly, the land of Canaan was always heavily influenced by the ideas and mythology of Mesopotamian civilization.

CHAPTER TEN
The Epic and the Flood

Of the more than two million discovered clay tablets with cuneiform writing, most are written in Akkadian, the language of Sumeria's conqueror, Sargon I. Akkadian became the basic language of Mesopotamia down through Babylonia, Assyria, the Neo-Babylonians (Chaldeans), and on to the Hurrians, who learned and used Akkadian but also kept their own unclassifiable language.

The world's oldest epic was first recorded in Sumeria, and it is the source of the *great flood story*. Unfortunately, only parts of two slightly different versions of the story have been found on Sumerian clay tablets. Perhaps the remaining pieces will be uncovered someday, and we will then know the Sumerian version in full.

Fortunately, the entire epic, under the name *Gilgamesh*, was carried down into Babylonian, Assyrian, and Hurrian times in Mesopotamia. The most nearly complete version of Gilgamesh existing today is preserved on 12 clay tablets from the library of the Assyrian king Ashurbanipal, which were retrieved from the ruins of Nineveh, his capital city. The first *Babylonian* version of the Sumerian flood story is at least 1,000 years older than the flood story as recounted in *Genesis*.

For many centuries, the Gilgamesh epic has been a part of the cultural foundation of Mesopotamia and the Middle East. It is still taught there in the curriculum of both public and private schools. We do Beowulf; they do Gilgamesh.

When I first encountered Beowulf in high school, I assumed that the fundamental purpose of an epic poem was to tell a good story. Now I understand that when an epic poem was carried down through generations of itinerant story tellers, it was meant to say to all who listened: *"This is who you are; this is who you should be."*

There are many different accounts of the Gilgamesh epic, including some 75 separate versions recorded on the oldest Babylonian tablets. The story goes something like this:

There is a handsome, feisty young king of the city of Uruk named Gilgamesh.[40] He built his city well, but worked his people ruthlessly. Gilgamesh was having a grand, disorderly time, when the somewhat jealous gods answer the pleas of his people to save them from their king. The goddess Ishtar asks Gilgamesh's creator—his grandmother, Aruru—to create wild man named Enkidu out of clay and spit. This hairy clay barbarian, equal in size and strength to Gilgamesh, becomes a friendly companion to all wild animals living in the woods. He sets out for Uruk to fight and kill Gilgamesh after hearing of the king's arrogant misbehavior.

On his way to Uruk, Enkidu encounters a hunter, whose son rushes to inform Gilgamesh of the gods' deadly plot. Gilgamesh decides to outfox them all. He sends a beautiful temple prostitute from the city to meet Enkidu. After a week of sensual pleasure, Enkidu has a new appreciation for the city, and gladly follows her into Uruk. (If you know the old Lil' Abner comic strip, you will understand that this courtesan has to be the first Stupefying Jones.) One of the Babylonian poets reworking this old set of Sumerian stories had fun with this scene, saying that when Enkidu pressed against the bosom of the courtesan, he forgot where he was born! In those days of individual city-states, that meant you had *really* lost it. But the poet had forgotten his own storyline: Enkidu wasn't born—he was created out of spit and clay. Well, we get the point. A country boy, or even a prodigal son, can be seduced by the city.

Enkidu and Gilgamesh fight, but Gilgamesh wins. They become close friends. Together, they go on a *hero's journey* to fight a monster who rules the sacred cedar trees. On their return, the lusty goddess Ishtar (*Inanna* in earlier Sumerian versions) decides that she wants to have Gilgamesh as a lover.

When Gilgamesh spurns her, she enlists the prevailing Babylonian deities to help her kill his friend Enkidu as an act of revenge. Before he dies, Enkidu shouts out a curse on all prostitutes, remembering that it was a temple courtesan who first tempted him into the city. The Babylonian sun god Shamash chides Enkidu for denouncing someone who had been helpful in so many ways. Enkidu dies of a simple illness and descends to the Babylonian netherworld *Irkalla*.

Enkidu wants to tell his friend Gilgamesh how terrible things are in the afterlife, so somehow he gets a three-day pass back to Uruk. Gilgamesh asks how things are down there in Irkalla, and Enkidu says that it is mostly bad news: All the residents of the underworld have to drink muddy water, even Gilgamesh's royal parents. Gilgamesh cries: *"Oh, give them clean water!"*

Everyone in Uruk wants to question Enkidu about their departed kin. In one tender passage—about the only sentimental one in this part of the epic, a young woman asks about the fate of her two stillborn children "who never knew existence." Enkidu replies: *"They play games at a table of gold and silver, and the table is laden with honey and clarified butter."* Someone even asks about a leper who died. Enkidu says: *"The leper's food is set apart; his water is set apart. He eats just outside the gates of Irkalla."* In other words, the leper is shunned, just as he had been in Uruk.

After Enkidu returns to the underworld, Gilgamesh grieves for him and the suffering of the dead. For the first time, Gilgamesh becomes deeply concerned over his own mortality. He remembers that a distant relative Utnapishtim knows the secret of eternal life. Again, Gilgamesh goes on a *hero's journey*, this time to find Utnapishtim, the original Noah.

In one Old Babylonian version of the epic, Gilgamesh gets aid and advice from a tavern keeper/wine goddess named SIDURI, the *refresher*. (In the Hurrian language, the word *Siduri* meant *young woman.*) She argues against his search for immortality. Noting that each of us will die someday, she offers Gilgamesh this bit of wisdom:

> *"Fill your belly with good things; day and night, night and day, dance and be merry, feast and rejoice. Let your clothes be fresh, bathe yourself in warm water, cherish the young child that takes your hand, take your wife joyful in your embrace; for this too is the lot of man."*[41]

Gilgamesh rejects Siduri's advice, crosses the *waters of death* with the aid of the ferryman, and finds his lost relative Utnapishtim. The Sumerians were the first to tell the story of the *Great Flood*. In their version of the epic, they gave the original Noah the name *Ziusudra*. The Old Babylonians kept the story pretty much intact, but changed the name of the ark-builder from Ziusustra to Utnapishtim.

Utnapishtim had been cleverly warned by the god Ea that the great god Enlil was planning a deluge to rid the earth of all those noisy, rapidly reproducing people and, for good measure, all other living creatures. Utnapishtim is given the dimensions for the ark, and he constructs it faithfully. He takes on board the ark his family and only one pair of all the animals, both wild and domesticated.

In addition—and note this—Utnapishtim takes on board at least one each of all types of craftsmen, so that civilization might be preserved. That superb idea should have been kept in the Old Testament. Perhaps the Hebrew writers had already decided on Cain as the one to be charged with building the cities, after slaying his brother, Abel.

Mesopotamia was a land that knew floods, but these were not necessarily from local rainfall; floods most often came down the rivers from heavy rainfall in distant mountains. The Gilgamesh epic gives this account:

> "For six days and six nights the wind blew, torrent and tempest and flood overwhelmed the world, tempest and flood raged together like warring hosts..."[42]

After only six days of windstorm and flood, and only a seventh day and seventh night for the ark to float peacefully on the water, Utnapishtim begins to send out birds. The first was a dove, and the dove returns. Then a swallow, and that returns. Finally a raven is sent out, but the raven does not return. The ark lands on top of a high mountain.

The epic continues beyond the flood story and recounts a challenge remarkably similar to the Old Testament's Garden of Eden story. Gilgamesh finds Utnapishtim after a perilous journey across the sea of death. Utnapishtim tries to convince Gilgamesh that eternal life is not at all what it is cut out to be—it is so boring! Finally, the secret is given: There is a forbidden plant growing at the bottom of the sea. When the plant is eaten, one gains eternal life.

Gilgamesh dives into the sea, with rocks on his feet to help him reach the bottom, and obtains some of the forbidden plant. He vows to take it back to Uruk where, with proper ceremony, he will consume it and gain everlasting life. However, on his way home Gilgamesh decides to rest. Would you believe it? A serpent comes along and eats all the forbidden plant. The serpent promptly sheds its skin and cheats mankind out of eternal life. Note that there was no blame placed on a woman. If anyone made a mistake, it was a man.

Gilgamesh, now an older and wiser king matured by his experiences, returns home with the realization that his only hope for immortality is to make his city, Uruk, a splendid place. Well, not quite his only reason to hope. He could become the central figure of the world's first epic poem!

CHAPTER ELEVEN
Proverbial Wisdom

Proverbs were very important to Mesopotamian civilization because, like epic poems, this *wisdom literature*
reminded individuals of the kind of person they were supposed to be. The Sumerians recorded more proverbs than
any other ancient people. One archaeologist working in the
ruins of three Sumerian cities found 15 collections of proverbs in 10 different books-on-tablets, with the oldest dating
to 2686 BCE.

Two of these collections were similar to those in the
Old Testament book of *Proverbs*, which is often attributed to Solomon. Biblical scholars suggest that the com-
pilers of *Proverbs* used two different sets of folk adages,
one of which had 375 entries. It is the one most similar

to a Sumerian collection of 365 proverbs. Here are some Sumerian examples:[43]

> When righteousness ends, injustice increases.
> Sweet words (compliments) are everyone's friend.
> Writing is the mother of speech, and the father of learning.
> If you know, why not teach someone!
> Tell a lie now, and everything that you say after that will be counted as a lie!
> Accept your lot and make your mother happy.
> Respect your mother as if she were divine.
> To be sick is acceptable; to be pregnant is painful; but to be pregnant and sick is just too much.
> Strength cannot keep pace with intelligence.
> A troubled mind makes you ill.
> For his pleasure, he got married. On thinking it over, he got divorced.
> Wealth is hard to come by, but poverty is always at hand.
> The poor are the silent ones of the land.
> All the households of the poor are not equally submissive.
> A poor man does not strike his son a single blow; he treasures him forever.

His destruction is from his own personal god; he knows no savior.
Whoever has walked with truth generates life.
"Give me!" is what the king says.
In a city without a guard dog, the fox is the inspector.
(That must have had a double meaning!)

Of particular interest is a Sumerian clay tablet punched with a stylus to produce cuneiform writing in 2100 BCE. (That is about 1,400 years before any of the Bible was written in forms we know.) It is called the *Shuruppak Instructions.*[44]

The opening lines of the *Shuruppak Instructions* might win the annual Bulwer-Lytton Fiction Contest today. (The English Department of San Jose State University awards a prize to the author who composes the worst first sentence of a novel.) However, when the *Shuruppak Instructions* were written, this was the call of the wandering story teller, settling his audience around him in the town square:

"In those days, in those far remote days, in those nights, in those faraway nights, in those years, those far remote years, at that time the wise one who knew how to speak in elaborate words lived in the Land; Shuruppak, the wise

one, who knew how to speak with elaborate words lived in the Land."

The *Instructions* were words of advice from a father to his son, but the genealogy is relevant to our chapter dealing with the great flood. The tablet is named after King Shuruppak, ruler of an ancient Sumerian city. His father was Ubara-Tutu, listed on the Sumerian Kings List as the last king before the flood. Shuruppak must have been king during that event because his son, for whom the *Instructions* were written, was none other than Ziusudra, the Sumerian *Noah*.

A city some 35 miles southeast of Nippur was named Shuruppak, after this king, but his reputation as a source of wisdom has lasted longer than his namesake city. The clay tablet containing the most nearly complete set of *Shuruppak's Instructions* was found comparatively recently, in 1963, in the ruins of that city.

Sometimes referred to as the Abu Salabikh Tablet, after the Arab name for the mound or *tell* from which it was excavated, it was instantly copied and translated by the Oriental Institute of Chicago. That was fortunate for us. However, the tablet was one of the many irreplaceable items housed in the Iraq National Museum that disappeared during looting in 2003. The tablet has not been recovered.

Shuruppak's *Instructions* to his son had five of the Ten Commandments, including not taking sacred names in vain, not killing anyone, or doing those things that lead to adultery, stealing, or the bearing of false witness.

Four of his wise counsels are quite similar to ones found in the Old Testament book of *Proverbs*. Two are quite long and are found in *Proverbs* 6:1-5 and 7:21-27. The first of those advises against a pledge of service to a neighbor; the second against entanglement with a wicked woman. The shorter two are found in *Proverbs* 22:26-27 and 23:27-28: The first warns against pledging for another's debts, and the second is a dire warning against consorting with a prostitute.

There is another reason why these fatherly counsels are interesting. The Shuruppak *Instructions* were written during a time of cultural revival led by the city of Ur, after Sumeria had experienced some 200 years of subordination to patriarchal Akkadians. In that context, it is interesting to note the cautionary words this father gives to his son about women, generally, and in particular, the sometimes questionable rationale for the advice:

> You should not play around with a married young woman: The slander could be serious. My son, you should not even sit alone in a chamber with a married woman.

You should not rape someone's daughter: The court-yard will learn of it!

You should not have sex with your slave girl: She will chew you up!

You should not buy a prostitute: She has a mouth that bites!

You should not buy a palace slave girl: She will always be the bottom of the barrel!

You should not abduct a wife: You should not make her cry.

You should not choose a wife during a festival. Her inside is an illusion; her outside is an illusion. The silver on her is borrowed; the jewelry on her is borrowed. The dress on her is borrowed; the linen garment on her is borrowed.

Your elder sister is indeed like a mother. You should be obedient to your elder sister as if she were your mother.

At harvest time, at that most priceless time, collect like a slave girl, but eat like a queen; my son, this is how it should be."

An early homophobia is noted, as well:

"You should not establish a home with an arrogant man: He will make your life like that of a slave girl. You will not be able to travel through any human dwelling without being shouted at: "There you go! There you go!"[45]

CHAPTER TWELVE
Something Borrowed...

It is doubtful that the Sumerians were the first to organize religion into a form we would recognize, but 5,000 years ago, they *were* the first to write about it. Almost certainly, the Sumerians get credit for concepts and stories that were developed by even earlier people. They often refer formally to places and persons of the past that were named in a language other than their own. They also borrowed ancient stories, convinced that the stories were theirs already. In terms of our understanding, that would make them the *100% Sumerians*.

Most of the time, when Hebrew writers borrowed ancient mythology, stories and religious ideas, they refined them aesthetically and spiritually, but they were still borrowing. Samuel Noah Kramer, the leading American scholar of Sumerology, argued emphatically that the Jews did not inherit these stories through their language—there were no linguistic parallels.

Unfortunately, in keeping with their own nomadic past, the Hebrew writers often made their borrowed stories more *patriarchal* than the Sumerian originals. In that regard, we need to remember that Mesopotamia, Egypt, and Canaan, had *goddesses* as well as gods. Those three areas exerted the strongest cultural influence on the Jews.

We are going to look at about 20 things that came into the Bible, in one way or another, from Sumerian culture. Samuel Kramer took the lead in identifying 15 of these in a chapter of his classic text, _The Sumerians: Their History, Culture, and Character._ The chapter was titled _"The Legacy of Sumer."_[46]

Kramer was a brilliant Sumerologist and a professor at the University of Pennsylvania. His book, _The Sumerians,_ was first published in 1963, and it reinforced Kramer's reputation as one of the world's principal authorities on this early civilization. He was so familiar with the relevant archaeological finds that he often paired fragments of Sumerian cuneiform tablets housed in American museums in Chicago or Philadelphia with matching fragments he found housed in museums in London, Berlin or Ankara.

Some of the themes and ideas borrowed from Sumeria by later Hebrew writers were first translated from tablets by Kramer; others had been discovered and translated as early as the 1890s, and even more in the first decades of the 20th

Century before Kramer completed most of his translations. As a prelude to the list of borrowings for the Old Testament, let's look at these two pertinent comments by Kramer from the early 1960s:[47]

> "In the course of the third millennium BC, the Sumerians developed religious ideas and spiritual concepts that left an indelible impression on the modern world, especially by way of Judaism, Christianity, and Mohammedism [i.e., Islam]...

> "The Sumerians, according to their own records, cherished goodness and truth, law and order, justice and freedom, righteousness and straightforwardness, mercy and compassion, and naturally abhorred their opposites..."

Now, largely following Kramer, let's examine some themes and stories familiar in the Old Testament that appear more than a 1,000 years earlier in ancient religious traditions:

1. The Sumerians believed that *a deep primordial sea had existed before creation*, and that same idea is expressed in *Genesis* written some 1,500 years later. (It helps to remember that the earth's surface is still 71% water.)

2. In the main Sumerian creation story, heaven and earth were brought up in one piece out of that primordial sea by the god Enki. But then Enlil, the Sumerian God of the Air, *blew through and separated heaven from the earth.*

Here's the beautiful version of that story in the Old Testament's *Genesis* 2,000 years later:

> *"In the beginning, when God created the heavens and the earth, the earth was a formless void, and darkness covered the face of the deep, while a wind from God swept over the face of the waters..."*

After the nomadic and Semitic Amorite people from the highlands to the west conquered most of Mesopotamia, they became, over time, the first Babylonians. To enthrone a supreme male god of their own, they introduced a new mythology by way of a creation epic known as *Enuma Elish*. In it, a gigantic, monstrous goddess named *TIAMAT* replaced the benign Sumerian Goddess *NAMMU* as the goddess of the primeval saltwater sea. Tiamat had a "sacred marriage" with *APSU*, Babylonian god of all freshwater beneath the surface of the earth.

From their union of salt and fresh water, Tiamat and Apsu were the parents of all other gods and goddesses. When their divine offspring became a nuisance, Tiamat and Apsu decided to do away with them. Their plans were overheard, and Apsu was killed in his sleep by the god Ea, and Tiamat was destroyed after a great battle by a new young god, *MARDUK*, son of Ea.

When Marduk sliced Tiamat into two parts, the upper half became the heavens, and the lower half became the earth. Marduk, associated with water, wisdom, and magic, moved to the top of the Babylonian hierarchy of deities. Quite naturally, Marduk was the patron deity of the city of Babylon.

As the Hebrew writers' concept of God had matured over time, it is easy to see why the gentle Sumerian versions of creation were preferred as a literary and spiritual model over the violent vision of the Babylonians. In fact, the Sumerian creation stories were preserved in Mesopotamia throughout Babylonian times and beyond by those temple priests and priestesses who found them to be more meaningful.

3. For the Sumerians and, much later, for the Hebrews, *mankind was fashioned from clay, and then imbued with the breath of life*. For both the Sumerians and the Hebrews, humans were created for the purpose of serving their god (or gods and goddesses.) As the Sumerian poetry tells us, human labor relieved the

lesser deities from having to work. For both groups, Sumerian and Hebrew, the seventh day of creation became a day of rest.

4.   According to Sumerian writers, creation was accomplished in two ways: by divine command through *naming the names* and by *shaping the materials of creation.* Two thousand years later, the Hebrew writers will include both of those descriptions of creation, in *Genesis.* (Early Egyptian mythology also presented the same two means of creation, long before *Genesis* was recorded.)

5.   The Sumerians had the idea of *a divine paradise* which they called Dilmun. Rivers flowed out of Dilmun in all directions. Most of the early Sumerian cities were located on a floodplain which early scholars recorded as E-D-I-N, Edin. Some modern scholars studying this same area have started identifying it as E-D-E-N, Eden.[48]

In the center of Dilmun, there was a tree of knowledge in which "*a serpent who could not be charmed made its nest in the roots of the ... tree ... And the dark maid Lilith built her home in the trunk.*" In this translation by Samuel Kramer, assisted by Diane Wolkstein, Kramer translated the Sumerian word *Lilitu* as Lilith, and there is no reason to believe this was incorrect.

In the Jewish *Midrash*, which contains a wide assortment of commentaries, anecdotes and folktales related to the Hebrew Bible, Lilith is the legendary first wife of Adam who refused to be subservient to him. Midrash writers believed that the Bible could not make an error, so when they saw those two different stories of creation in *Genesis*, they assumed that there were two different creations, with a cancellation in between.

For them, Lilith was indeed the woman in the first creation story. Not only did she refuse to obey Adam, she refused to let Adam lie on top of her because he smelled like dirt. Adam sent her away.

In Sumeria, for a time, Lilith (as *Lilitu*) was referred to as the handmaiden of Inanna. Remember that after the staunchly patriarchal Babylonians took over from the more gender-balanced Sumerians, Inanna became Ishtar. In one role, Lilith may have been transformed into a provocative procurer of males for the prostitutes in Ishtar's temples.

Lilith is not mentioned in the Torah—the first five books of the Hebrew bible—or in the Christian Old Testament. Lilith as *Lilitu* does get a one-time mention in *Isaiah* 34-14, in the original Hebrew. However, the King James Bible translators did not know Sumerian, so when they got to that verse, they translated *Lilitu* as *Screech Owl*, which is how some Midrash writers referred to her. In drawings and sculpture, she is accompanied by two great owls, the Sumerian symbol for wisdom. The passage in *Isaiah* says that Lilith will find a home in the wilderness after God wreaks his vengeance on mankind.

The term *Talmud* refers to rabbinical commentaries on just about everything in Jewish culture. Two quite respectable reference sources say the Talmud mentions Lilith, and one quite respectable source says the Talmud does not. As there are two Talmuds, one written in Jerusalem and a longer one written in Babylon after the captivity, both sources may be correct.

As you may recall, the Torah was attributed to Moses, who was believed to be recording God's word in *Genesis*, *Exodus*, *Leviticus*, *Numbers*, and *Deuteronomy*. Reputable Biblical scholars are now confident that these books had a number of separate authors. In the Midrash stories, Lilith was expelled from the Garden of Eden for not being submissive to Adam. In Islamic mythology, with roots in Judaism, Lilith married the devil and became the mother of the Jinn, all the evil and mischievous spirits. Lilith is mentioned in one of the Dead Sea Scrolls as a devil.

In 2003 CE, for its 250th anniversary, the British Museum spent 1.5 million British pounds to purchase a famous terracotta bas-relief sculpture of Lilith.[49] It is called the Burney Relief, as it had been for a time in the hands of a British collector named George Burney.

Figure 20: Lilith, in the Burney Relief

Notice that Lilith has the feet and wings of a bird, so she truly can live in a tree. In each hand, interestingly, she holds a rod and a ring, which were symbols of authority and justice. She is referred to as Goddess of the Night by early clay tablet sources, and her stepped crown reflects various stages of the moon. At her feet are two lions, universal signs of strength and power, and she is accompanied by two owls, the Babylonian bird of wisdom.

The bas-relief sculpture is Babylonian, dated by the British Museum to about 1800 BCE. Originally bought in three pieces, with a few additional fragments, the fired-clay plaque has been carefully restored. One broken rod was not repaired.

6. In Sumerian mythology, there were many stories about *individuals with very long life-spans*. This idea was carried down by all the subsequent empires that occupied Mesopotamia, and then used by the Hebrew writers for their own purposes: Methuselah, 969 years; Noah, 950; and Adam, 930, for example. As noted earlier, in their king lists, the Sumerians beat them at that game, with claims of life-spans of thousands of years for some of their kings.

The Sumerians were more than a little short on reliable historical data, because they had just invented writing. Of course, they depended on extensive oral histories—some real, much imagined—that come with any early culture. Before and after the invention of writing, the cultivation of memory was a necessity for the preservation and transmission of all that mattered. After the invention of writing, the vast majority of the people remained illiterate, and good minds continued to develop amazing capacities for memorization.

7. As we noted earlier, the story of the Great Flood was a major part of the world's oldest epic, which we now know as Gilgamesh. *Ziusudra* was the Sumerian name for the original Noah, but the Old Babylonian name *Utnapishtim* was adopted about 1700 BCE.

The Assyrians, who came after the Babylonians, adopted the same story, as did their successors—the Neo-Babylonians, the Hittites, and the Hurrians. The Hurrians made only minor changes, but one was to give the Noah character the Hurrian name *Nahmizuli.*

It was the Hurrian version of the flood story that was borrowed for the story told by the Hebrew writers. There are minor differences in detail, but two of the paragraphs of the flood story in *Genesis* are nearly identical to corresponding paragraphs of the older Hurrian narrative. The name *Noah* may have been taken from the first part of the Hurrian name *Nahmizuli* because, in early Hebrew, Noah was written as *Nhm*.[50] Incidentally, Mount Ararat, where Noah's ark landed in the *Genesis* version, was inside Hurrian territory at the time of its recording.

8. *Tower of Babel.* As mentioned earlier, Sumerian temples were those layered, artificial mountains called ziggurats. By the time the Jews were brought

to Babylon in captivity, most of the old ziggurats were in ruins. These had been destroyed by time, not invasion or war. However, in the middle of their captivity in Babylon, the Jews got to experience the building of the very last ziggurat.

Nebuchadnezzar II had workers from many of the lands he had conquered, all speaking different languages, build a *seven-storied mountain,* the meeting of heaven and earth. His ziggurat was just over 300 feet high—in fact, very close to the height of the Texas State Capitol Building. We know the height of the ziggurat from the original architect's clay tablets that gave all the dimensions. (Texans remember the height of *their* state capitol building because, naturally, it was intentionally pushed to be just a little higher than the nation's capitol, which is an ample 289 feet.)

This last ziggurat was a temple dedicated to the god Marduk, the patron deity of Babylon. We know it as the *Tower of Babel*, as suggested in *Genesis* chapter 11. Among other things, the author is trying to explain why there are so many different languages in use on the earth. Interestingly, the Sumerian name of the last ziggurat was *Etemenanki*, or the *Foundation of Heaven and Earth.*

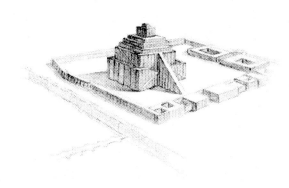

Figure 21: The last ziggurat, following the architect's written description.

9. The Sumerian god of wisdom was first named Enki, and then later became known by the Akkadians as Ea (Yah). In a very long poem called *"Enki and the World Order,"* Enki established all the earthly boundaries for all the many different groups of humans. The poem has 466 lines, but while the old Sumerian city of Nippur was being excavated around 1888, the large clay tablet with the poem broke in half. Unknowingly, one half went to a German university, and the other half to the University of Pennsylvania. Samuel Kramer identified the two pieces as parts of the same tablet in 1960.

In *Deuteronomy* 32: 7-14 there is an interesting verse that says: *"When the Most High apportioned the nations, when he divided mankind, he fixed the boundaries of the peoples according to the number of the gods; the Lord's own portion was his people."*

10. Sumerians were the first to declare that there was a *Most High God*, with six powerful deities supporting him, and many lesser gods. The early writers of the Old Testament would occasionally suggest that there were lesser gods, subject to the *Most High God*. Eventually, after an experience in Egypt, they would finally declare that there was only one god, their God.

11. Sometime around 2500 BCE, the Sumerians created the concept of a *personal god,* but originally this was only for men. Then, about 300 years later, priestesses worshipping the Goddess of Heaven, Inanna, expanded the concept to include women as well. A personal god was a loving god. The relationship with a personal god often involved a vision or a dream which resulted in an understanding or covenant similar to the one understood by the Hebrews with Yahweh.

We should note that, in Sumerian mythology, it was Inanna, the Goddess of Heaven and Earth, who made the first covenant with all mankind. Through her high priestesses, Inanna said that if human beings would be righteous, there would never again be a Great Flood.[51] In the much later flood story in Genesis, God makes a covenant with the Hebrew people promising that there will never again be a Great Flood.

12. In his book, _The Sumerians_, Samuel Kramer states explicitly that the _moral codes and ethical concepts_ of the Sumerians were identical to those adopted so much later by the Hebrew writers of the Old Testament. Then later, he waffled a bit and suggested that maybe the Sumerians were not _quite_ as high-minded or as morally fervent as the Hebrews. To be fair, the Hebrew writers had at least 1,000 years for thoughtful development of these ideas.

13. As suggested earlier, Sumerian city laws were the basis for all subsequent law codes in the Mesopotamian cultural area, including the famous one by the Babylonian king Hammurabi composed about 1700 BCE. We noted that the two most advanced Sumerian cities, Ur and Lagash, had moved away from _equivalent retribution_—an eye for an

eye, a tooth for a tooth—almost 500 years before Hammurabi's law code, and 1,000 years before the early Hebrew law codes were written down.

Recently, some commentators on harsh penalties in the Torah—the first five books of the Old Testament—have tried to argue that the verses did not really mean *eye for an eye;* instead, they actually meant *monetary damages.* My reading is that the Old Testament meant exactly what it said, just as Hammurabi meant what he said, and all the law code makers before him. They spelled it out!

Interestingly enough, the cities of Ur and Lagash had come up with monetary damages more than 1,000 years before the Old Testament. However, the law codes of those two Sumerian cities specified exactly what those monetary damages were to be for each offense—no guessing as to what was meant, or whether they meant it.

14. The notion of *divine retribution* was a familiar Sumerian theme, and was incorporated ▬▬ much later in the Old Testament. In Sumeria, that usually meant a Sumerian deity allowing a devastating attack by some neighboring people in response to the sinful behavior of the Sumerian people, or in response to a blasphemous act by a Sumerian ruler. Both of these scenarios are familiar themes in the Old Testament.

Yet, in one early Sumerian myth which certainly does not make it into the Old Testament, the Goddess Inanna is taken advantage of, sexually, by an exceptionally gifted gardener who had cultivated a marvelously large tree. Inanna stops to rest in the shade of the tree, and goes to sleep. When Inanna wakes up and realizes what the gardener has done to her, she sends a series of plagues against the entire land.

The first of Inanna's plagues was to fill up all the wells and drinking places with blood. (In the Old Testament tradition, this was the first plague visited on the Egyptians for not letting God's people go.) The second of Inanna's plagues was a sweeping, destructive wind followed immediately by a flood.

The third plague was an interesting one: It blocked completely all roads and highways carrying people and goods. That would have brought the economy to an abrupt halt. Inanna only sent three plagues; Yahweh hit the Egyptians with 10. And earlier we mentioned the Great Flood—the archetypal story of divine retribution—and that was also Sumerian in origin, elaborated on by almost everybody.

15. *Moses in the basket* story. As we noted earlier, the first people to conquer the Sumerians were the Akkadians under Sargon I, who put together the world's first empire. The story of his origin was that he was an illegitimate baby placed in a basket made of reeds that had been waterproofed with

pitch, and then floated down to where the royal family was having a picnic. Sargon is found by a princess, who raises him. He ultimately becomes the leader of the nation. That popular Sargon story is about 1,000 years older than the one given for Moses.

16. *Trials of Job* story. One of the outstanding poetic tales in Sumerian and Babylonian literature is about a wealthy, righteous man who suddenly loses everything—his family, his wealth, his health. He is reduced to begging at the city gates, covered with sores.

His friends think he has committed some secret sin; others say that if he will just trust in the gods, everything will be all right. He appeals to his personal deity for help. The Sumerians called him Balta-atrua or, in some tablets, Laluralim. The Babylonians called him Tabu-utul-Bel. In the Old Testament, he is called Job.

In the Babylonian poems, which are longer than the Sumerian creations, the Job character offers prayers in the temple of his god, but manages also to take flour to the temple of his *goddess* for making bread for the poor.[52] In both the Sumerian and Babylonian stories, all is restored in the end, as the gods stop testing his faith.

For the Old Testament, the Hebrew writers created in the story of Job a deeper and more thoughtful literary masterpiece of prose and poetry. The early mention of Satan in *Job* 1:6 suggests quite strongly that it was written after the Babylonian Captivity ended in 538 BCE. In Babylon, the captive Hebrews had their first encounter with Zoroastrianism, a religion that strongly emphasized the battle between good and evil.

17. The Sumerians, or a people before them copied by the Sumerians, gave us the idea of a *netherworld* as a physical place, an *abode of the dead* which they originally called *Kur*. (As noted earlier, the Babylonians changed the name of that underworld to *Irkalla*.)

18. From the start, the Sumerians and all who built on their culture believed in angels. The angels were *winged messengers* serving the gods and goddesses. Over time, this Mesopotamian belief in angels would be expanded to the notion that every human being had a guardian angel. But it would be the Zoroastrians who first named the major angels—Gabriel, Michael, and Raphael.

19. Many of you will remember Bill Moyers' television special on *Genesis*, a number of years ago. Instead of starting with creation, he began with the Cain and

Abel story. If you recall, Cain (the farmer) killed his brother Abel (the shepherd). This was one of the longest-running pieces of symbolic mythology in Mesopotamia, beginning with the Sumerians: the conflict between the settled farmer and the nomadic shepherd.

Rather than stealing birthrights, however, in Sumeria the farmer and shepherd are fighting for the love of the goddess Inanna, or for one of her many later incarnations—Ishtar, Ashtoreth, and right down to Astarte and Aphrodite for the Greeks, and Venus for the Romans.

Early on, nomadic invaders who conquered the city states would side with the shepherd, who would win the struggle with the farmer in their stories. Dwellers in the cities sympathized with the farmer who, after all, made cities possible with his surplus food. We should probably note that the shepherd god evolved over time into the god of agriculture, so in the end he had both camps covered.

The shepherd god's Sumerian name was *Dumuzzi*, and that morphed into *Tammuz* under Sumeria's Akkadian conquerors. (His name was also Tammuz in Babylonian, Assyrian, and other cultures adopting the Akkadian language.) Tammuz is trapped in the underworld, but his lover Inanna, Goddess of Heaven,[53] gets a brief reprieve for him in the spring of each year so he and Inanna can mate together and assure a successful harvest. For about 11 months of the year, Tammuz is separated from his lover. This story made the women living in Mesopotamian cultural areas break down and cry for Tammuz just thinking about it.

Some 1,200 years after the Babylonians wrote down their version, the Hebrew god is angry and, as they say, isn't going to take it anymore. He sends a terrible apparition to point out to the prophet Ezekiel all kinds of ongoing wickedness. One notable abomination was that the women of Jerusalem were still participating in a competing religion. *Ezekiel 8:14* records the scene: *"Then he brought me to the door of the gate of the LORD'S house which was toward the north; and behold, there sat the women weeping for Tammuz."*

And then the ghostly figure shows Ezekiel 25 men with their backs to the temple, worshipping the sun. (Some days are just harder than others in the prophesy business.) However, things could get a lot worse. Ezekiel would soon witness the destruction of Jerusalem, and be taken in captivity to Babylon.

20. *Periodic relief from oppressive debt* originated in early Mesopotamia. Lending money at interest to merchants and to farmers who owned land had become a common practice in early Sumeria. Students in the school for scribes did computational

exercises to determine when a loan would become so large that it could never be repaid.

On default, the debtor's household goods were taken first, and then any other possessions, such as a merchant's store and boat, or a farmer's animals and land. In the next round, members of the families were taken as debt-slaves. The merchants and the farmers were the last to be taken as debt-slaves.

The increased probability of social unrest prompted by such conditions led the best of Sumerian kings to declare a periodic general amnesty from debts. As might be expected, rulers of the city of Lagash were early providers of 'clean-slate' debt relief, including the return of confiscated property to its original owners. Among them, King Urukagina and King Gudea were celebrated for their benevolence in declaring such periodic releases from long-term liabilities.

Archaeologists from the German Oriental Society working in north-central Turkey have found some 30,000 clay tablets, most of them from the ruins of Hattusa, the ancient Hittite capital. One set of tablets, found in both the Hurrian and Hittite languages, deals with debt remission. The Hurrians and Hittites got these ideas from the Babylonians, who were inspired by the earlier Sumerians, who called their debt-relief proclamations *declarations of freedom.*

Chapter 25 of *Leviticus* closely follows the earlier Hittite and Hurrian texts found at Hattusa. Leviticus gives a detailed prescription for declaring the Jubilee Year of debt relief as the 50th year, following seven cycles of seven years.[54]

As in the flood story, the Hurrian texts provided most of the borrowed material. Harry Hoffner, the great Hittite scholar of Chicago's Oriental Institute, commented that these old texts echoed biblical themes.[55] However, as it was the Sumerians who gave the first loud cry for justice and fairness, perhaps it was the Bible that sounded the echo. According to Hoffner:

"The people of ancient Israel left us a priceless treasure in the writings of the Hebrew Bible and the Greek New Testament. Because the narratives of the Bible are familiar to us from church and synagogue, we often unconsciously divorce them from their ancient roots.

"We do this because we value their teachings as expressions of timeless truth. But it is a mistake to fail to see that the particular forms of expressing these timeless truths can be associated with particular groups of people in specific geographical and chronological settings."

Amen.

CHAPTER THIRTEEN
That Country along the Nile

We are going to continue our look at the probable origin of certain ideas and passages found in the Old Testament, but we shift from Mesopotamia to Egypt. It is not easy to make a clean break here, because Mesopotamia and Egypt exchanged people, goods and ideas over the centuries.

In fact, over some 2,000 years, Egypt was settled by Semitic tribes who came in waves into the Nile Valley from Mesopotamia. That is rather ironic because all Semitic people first developed in a wetter North Africa, moved east, and then some came back at least part of the way.

The Cave of the Swimmers featured in the movie, *The English Patient*, was a real archaeological find near Egypt's border with Libya. (And yes, it *was* found by the Hungarian explorer László Almásy.) The cave's paintings of people swimming were created about 10,000 years ago, when things were a great deal wetter in that part of Egypt.

Somewhere around 7,000 BCE, a wave of Semitic immigrants from the wetter coastal regions of the Arabian Peninsula came to settle along the Nile. They only knew field cultivation, so they added little or nothing to farming practices along that great valley. However, about 5,000 BCE, the Nile valley was overrun by a different group of Semitic people coming in from Mesopotamia, and they introduced simple irrigation techniques.

A similar group from Mesopotamia arrived around 4,200 BCE. This last great wave of Semitic immigrants brought knowledge of many irrigation advances that had developed along the valleys of the Tigris and Euphrates rivers. Egypt's own Semitic language was developing at that time, but all this was happening before writing had been invented. There are no written records.

What we may surmise is that Egypt's civilization was jump-started and advanced at a faster rate and to higher levels than Sumeria ever knew. Egypt had a leap forward, culturally, in what it made and what it built. Ideas and technology were imported successfully, and Egypt soon outstripped Sumeria in almost all endeavors.

Over time, there were other invasions and in-migrations. The Egyptian gene pool was a marvel. Besides the dominant early Semitic groups, there were genetic inputs from two groups of black people to the south: Nubians from the

Sudan, and Abyssinians from present-day Ethiopia. To the east was Canaan, and the Canaanites were mostly brown-skinned Semitic people with ample mixing from other diverse groups. Over time, these would include Egyptian soldiers who marched into Canaan on many occasions.

Egypt also had early invasions by fair-skinned, blue-eyed people from the west, from present day Libya. Most likely, they were the descendants of Norse sailors who had ship-wrecked along the Libyan coast. The end result of all of this long period of mixing was that Egyptian babies were always shown on wall-paintings to be fair skinned at birth. However, as they grew older, they were depicted as tanned by the Egyptian sun to a pronounced copper color.

In 1289 BCE, Egypt was ruled by the Pharaoh Seti I. He ruled just before Rameses II while the Hebrew people were still in Egypt. In the tomb of Seti I was a wall painting of the Egyptians and all of their neighbors. The artist identified each group by their location with respect to Egypt and drew them, along with a group labeled *Egyptians*. The figure below begins and ends with two Canaanites. The four Egyptians are on the lower panel, front and center.

The figures are all males, but we understand the intent. Each group has handsome and dignified members, different only in their appearance. Skin color was not a major issue in Egypt; learning the Egyptian language and accepting Egyptian beliefs, customs, and rituals were very large issues for newcomers.

**Figure 22: Egyptians and their neighbors
(painted panel in tomb of Seti I)**

Several years ago, I was reading one of the better modern histories of Egypt. It was written by P. J. Vatikiotis.[56] However, I almost dropped the book when I read his comment that, if one traveled across the Nile valley, one would hardly notice where the green ends and the brown and yellow began.

Of course, it is all in the eye of the beholder but, for me, this is somewhat like going to the Grand Canyon and not noticing that there is a hole in the ground. The contrast between the thin strip of cultivated land and that desolate desert is dramatic. Abraham's family and, then later, Jacob's family and many others headed for the immense fertility of the valley of the Nile. Particularly, they went to the Nile's great delta, when they could no longer survive severe drought in Canaan.

The Nile itself was even more a part of Egyptian society and culture than the Tigris-Euphrates was for the Sumerians. In Mesopotamia, not only were there two major rivers involved, there were also a number of other rivers and streams helping make up these systems. And Mesopotamia had more semi-arid areas, with some seasonal rainfall along the main courses of the rivers. Some farmers were able to grow a rain-fed crop of barley. Not so in Egypt. Except for a few spring-fed oases and very sparse precipitation, the Nile was the only source of water, and water was necessary for life to flourish.

For most of the Nile's course through Egypt, until it reaches the delta around Alexandria, there is only the river, a narrow strip of irrigated land on each side, and the desert. At some places, you could hardly run a good 100-yard dash at right angles to the river, and still be in farmland. Fortunately, the valley does widen periodically, and then finally the river fans out through many tributaries over its broad, flat delta as the Nile approaches the Mediterranean.

Normally, in June, the Nile began its slow rise from rain and snowmelt in the highlands of Abyssinia—the old name for Ethiopia. By the end of August, most of the fields were flooded with water that carried fertilizing silt.[57] Before then, in preparation, there were the tasks of digging or plowing. The farmers in Egypt are still called *fellahin*, literally *soil-breakers*—the ones who prepare the soil for planting.

When the plots were too small to plow with an ox, or if the farmer was too poor to own or rent an ox, the land was dug by hand. Then, after planting seeds came the critically important task of trapping enough water to grow the crop to maturity.

The *fellah* and other able-bodied members of his family dug out a basin for storing flood water, or dug and maintained a gravity-fed canal, or lifted water manually for up to 16 hours a day—whatever it took to provide moisture for crops during the growing season. This life-or-death undertaking was a common experience for Egyptian farm families.

By late April or early May, the river was at its lowest level, and the crops had been harvested. Looking at the barren desert on either side of the Nile, you can understand why the *fellahin* thought that the desert was *overpopulated with demons* and *ruled by a demon*. That demon's name was *SETH*. (There is no particular reason to think there is a direct connection between this Seth and the Seth who would be recorded much later as Adam and Eve's third son, but the name choice is interesting.)

Like the Sumerians, the Egyptians developed a highly advanced city-based society, made possible by the surplus food produced by their farmers. However, in some meaningful ways, the cities in Egypt were different from the cities in Sumeria. Along the narrow valley of the Nile, there was a continuous, almost urban concentration of people between cities, for more than 600 miles.

In a very real way, the whole Nile Valley was the Pharaoh's operational city. It was a tightly constrained area. To the east and west, it was walled-in by the desert. To the south, away from the river, there was more desert, and then mountains. To the north was the Mediterranean Sea. All these barriers served as barriers to both out-migration and in-migration. And to some extent, these barriers were natural defenses against invasion by land.

Cities were scattered along the Nile, but were rarely in sight of each other because their dense agricultural support areas were long and extended down the narrow valley of the river. Back in Sumeria, if Abraham had been permitted to climb to the top of the ziggurat in Ur, he would have seen the ziggurats of four other cities.

In Sumeria, compact city-states seeking to expand their territorial control dominated the early scene. In Egypt, the primary purpose of the city was to serve as a control center for the nation, remembering that Upper and Lower (northern and southern) Egypt were first united as early as 3100

BCE. That makes early Egyptian cities somewhat more like early Chinese cities, which also served as national control centers during any period with a strong central government.

Also, in further contrast to Sumeria, Egyptian cities would become highly engaged in only a few productive activities—including weaving, metal-working, pottery-making, and jewelry assembly—serving the entire country. Egypt and the Egyptians adapted very well to such economic specialization. Those who concentrated on only one activity became very skilled at what they did. Given the opportunity, they could be exceptionally creative, and the palaces, temples, homes and tombs of the wealthy displayed the results.

The physical distribution of goods was not a major problem; the Nile was a convenient connector of all places along its banks. In Egypt's low-rainfall conditions, clay-topped roads alongside the Nile were quite serviceable for ox-drawn wagons. The clay often came from the maintenance of the irrigation canals, or from digging new ones. Ox-carts were particularly useful for moving goods upstream on short hauls to the south. On longer hauls in any direction, the oxen would eat up the profits. Light loads were carried short distances by men wearing shoulder yokes, and women carried water and other goods on their heads.

Boats, small ships, and rafts hauled most of the cargo going any distance downstream. To go upstream against the flow of the river was almost impossible during flood stage, but that was not a long period. At other times, boats with sails could move goods upstream. Sailing against the current was easier than moving up in society.

Social class was a serious issue for everyone from kings on down. At the bottom of the social pyramid were the slaves. Captured prisoners were often enslaved, but so were citizens of Egypt who broke certain laws or went too heavily into debt. Vassal states sent slaves to the Pharaoh as an inexpensive way to pay their annual tribute.

Hardly higher in status than the slaves were the landless laborers. These were serfs who assisted periodically on large farm plots owned by the temples, or who worked for nobles or merchants who owned farms. They were employed at very low wages by anyone who owned a farm larger than he or she could work alone.

Just above the landless serfs were the peasant farmers, the *fellahin*, who worked their own small plots of land. Much of the national food supply was provided by their hard work in the sun.

About equal to the fellahin in social standing were those serving in the lower ranks of the military, particularly after 1500 BCE when a standing army was first created in Egypt.

Next came the professional classes, including artists and artisans, and Egypt had many such vocations. From painters and sculptors to bas-relief artists, jewelers, and skilled workmen in all the construction trades, including boat-building, tomb construction, and the building of structures of every type imaginable. Artists and musicians, scribes, engineers, architects, physicians, and embalmers were all appreciated for their work.

Because of their ability to create wealth and make tax contributions, the merchants held on to the next higher social class, sandwiched between the professionals and the priests. The priests were powerful because of their constant role in religious rituals that also involved the Pharaoh, and because their temples controlled so much of the land and wealth of the nation.

The High Priests were not afraid to meddle in politics, including an occasional assassination, if they thought it was in their interest. Most of the officer corps came from the upper classes, so they held a social level about equal to that of the priesthood.

At the top of the social pyramid were the nobility, particularly the families of whatever dynasty was currently in power. Some overly cautious ruling families were weakened, genetically, by serious inbreeding. Male leaders married their nieces, their sisters, and unfortunately in some sad cases, their daughters.

Mummification was considered to be something more than the passport to eternity for the wealthy: *"You live again, you live again forever, you are young once more forever!"* When an upper-class Egyptian died, the mummifying process took

70 days—not because the embalmers needed the whole 70 days, but because 70 was an auspicious number. (And that stemmed from the old and popular appreciation for the number seven.)

One positive outcome of the Egyptian concern with health, the human body, and the afterlife was their amazing progress in medicine. The Egyptians were the best in the world for at least 2,000 years. It can be argued that the founder of modern medicine was not the Greek Hippocrates, but the Egyptian *Imhotep.* He lived about 2700 BCE and seemed to have had all the Sumerian medical knowledge, plus much more from Egypt.

Figure 23: IMHOTEP

Imhotep helped train specialists in obstetrics, gynecology, internal medicine (especially in gastric disorders), and in many surgical specialties. Imhotep was also an architect, and was in charge of building the first pyramid— the Step Pyramid of Zoser at Saqqara.

In 1600 BCE, 1,000 years after Imhotep and while the Hebrew people were in Egypt, a papyrus scroll was entombed that reviewed 48 very different surgical cases, with all necessary procedures described in great detail. The scroll specified that control of the body resided in the organ that we call the brain—the first recorded introduction of that concept. An earlier scroll listed 700 specific remedies for 700 specific ailments.

(One bizarre remedy is still stuck in my mind, but I've forgotten what it was supposed to cure. You probably wouldn't want to use it anyway, since it was composed of *lizard blood and crocodile dung, mixed well with mother's milk*. If your constitution got past the cure, you might even survive the ailment.)

Much later, there are records of Persia having sent a ship to Egypt to pick up a particular Egyptian eye surgeon to operate on Cyrus the Great for cataracts in about 525 BCE. Herodotus visited Egypt during Greek classical times, about 450 BCE, and wrote: *"The Egyptians suppose that all diseases to which people are subject proceed from the food they use."* A later Roman visitor wrote: *"The Egyptians believe that the larger part of the food taken into the body is superfluous, and it is from the superfluous part that diseases arise."*

Egyptian priests had a number of food avoidances, including pork and scaly fish. Some of the Jewish concerns about food must have come from their 430-year stay in Egypt, where a large number of foods were already suspect.

There is one particular element of early Egyptian culture, so dominant and profound, that it has led many scholars to declare that of the four great early civilizations—Mesopotamian, Egyptian, Indian, and Chinese—the greatest was the Egyptian. That element is art, including three-dimensional and bas-relief sculpture, painting, architecture, music and literature. It is from their painting that we have learned the most about this culture.

Even in a dry climate, anything written on papyrus did not last very long, unless it was placed in a container and then sealed, as was sometimes done. Fortunately for us, the priests decided rather early that you didn't have to stock the tombs with real supplies, but could paint them on the walls instead. Artists in great number were employed to decorate the walls of the tombs. Once the tombs were sealed, the paintings were surprisingly well preserved.

The result is an amazingly complete record of the entire life of the society in the tombs of the kings and their families, the nobility, wealthy merchants, top court administrators, and senior professionals. Every step of the agricultural process was depicted: plowing, raking, planting, irrigating, fertilizing, weeding, harvesting, milling, and storing. This was accompanied by illustrated recipes for preparing and cooking the food, and directions for serving the food properly. There are similarly detailed instructions for animal husbandry, weaving, mining, fishing, ale-making, smelting, and more.

There are even cartoons related to the life of the common people, but no cartoons of the upper crust. Whenever male rulers and nobles were depicted, they were most often hunting, fishing, fighting or dead. Women were more gently treated, and more accurately portrayed.

At least part of the explanation for that lies in the fact that, in Egypt, wealth was passed down along the female line—from a mother to a daughter or, if need be, to a sister or a niece. If you married inside the family, you kept the wealth inside the family.

One early piece of writing by a young merchant said that his father helped him operate his boat, but his mother bought it for him! In her book, The Egyptians, Barbara Watterson quipped that Egyptians passed property down the female line because they understood that maternity was a fact, but paternity was only an opinion.[58]

You will remember that the last two waves of agricultural migrants came into early Egypt from Mesopotamia, where goddesses were important deities. As a consequence, Egypt was one of the few societies in which a general equality of the sexes was actually practiced for most of its history. In fact, early Egypt came surprisingly close to being a matriarchal society.

An Egyptian woman was free to go wherever she wished, without an escort. She could go shopping alone and dine alone in public. She did not wear a veil over her face, normally. If she did, it was only to be in fashion. We know that by choice most Egyptian women stayed at home to raise their families. It was particularly important to them to have a mature, surviving daughter, given the inheritance patterns within Egyptian society.

Of course, that meant that Egyptian men held most of the jobs that required daily work outside the home. Most of the roles in the practice of religion went to men—probably because the temple was one place where wealth was not under the control of women. However, there were women priests as well. A few were even listed as high priests, but that was less common.

Certainly, upper class women could own and manage estates, just as lower class women worked in the fields alongside their husbands. Some women were educated as scribes, and some became skilled artisans in the many craft and construction workshops throughout the country. Women could transfer property, engage in commerce and manufacturing, and travel as their responsibilities required with an unusual degree of safety.

Pharaoh Rameses III, who became king in 1184 BCE, went to the trouble of having an inscription cut into stone, complimenting himself for keeping women safe while they traveled. The inscription read:

> "I enabled the woman of Egypt to go her own way, her journeys extended wherever she wanted, without anyone assaulting her on the road."

About the same time, however, a scribe offered this advice to his son concerning women who traveled:

> "Be on guard against a woman from abroad, who is not known in town. Above all, do not have sex with her."

We know that in the Egyptian royal court, princesses had tutors who educated them far beyond basic literacy. Nearly all lower class women were illiterate, as were the men. There are early references to female physicians, which meant that they were both well-educated and professionally trained. Women could enter into business contracts and make contracts for marriage and divorce. As in Sumeria, women could demand prenuptial agreements in defense of their interests.

Women could bring lawsuits to pursue their interests, and could appeal if they lost the first round of the court case. They often won on appeal. Most important, women could serve as witnesses in court with a standing equal to men. That was the litmus test for women's rights in early societies.

In court, a woman could represent herself or represent others. She did not have to have a male representative in court, as the Greeks would require much later. If an Egyptian wife divorced her husband, she kept all her dowry. If he divorced her, she not only kept her dowry, she got an additional settlement.

But there were some less commendable situations that we easily recognize. One letter by a divorced woman complained that after her husband received a major promotion, he dropped her and took a younger, prettier wife more in keeping with his new and higher position in society. And that describes the *trophy wife* phenomenon as we know it today. In spite of all that, most Egyptian women fared quite well.

About 500 BCE, a Greek visitor to Egypt joked that Egyptian men were hen-pecked. A few centuries later, a Roman visitor quipped that in Egyptian marriages, the groom had to promise to obey the bride. What both travelers realized was that women were more independent in Egypt than they were in their own countries, and perhaps theirs was nervous laughter.

This situation may very well have bothered Egyptian men, as well. One of the early Egyptian proverb writers, Ptah-Hotep, gave this note of advice to his son:

"Love your wife, clothe her, and make her happy—but don't let her get the upper hand!"[59]

Even though gender was seldom a troublesome issue in Egypt, the ruling monarch was nearly always a man. One enterprising woman, Queen Hatshepsut, declared herself to be the king as well as the queen. In spite of some attempts to suggest otherwise, Hatshepsut really was the wicked step-mother of Pharaoh Thutmose III.

While she was appointed regent to rule in his place only until he became of age, Hatshepsut occupied his throne and ruled for almost 22 years until her death in 1458 BCE. She was the fifth Pharaoh of Egypt's 18th dynasty, and was known for her intelligence and wisdom.

Hatshepsut's reign occurred during the time the Hebrew people were enslaved in Egypt. Some may have seen Hatshepsut appear on the balcony of her palace, waving to the people below. She wore the clothes of a traditional male pharaoh and a fake beard to remove any lingering doubts as to whether she was the ruler of Egypt. In spite of that ploy, a variety of sculptures show her to be an attractive woman.

Figure 24: Hatshepsut

Hatshepsut wrote this about herself: *"I am exceedingly good to look upon....a beautiful maiden....fresh, serene of nature....altogether divine!"*

She even orchestrated a new mythology concerning her birth, claiming that the god *AMUN* had assumed the role of *father* in her conception. That may have helped in securing priestly support for a woman in the role of pharaoh. However, what is most remembered about her reign is the astounding number of public buildings that were completed.

That includes her own mortuary complex at Deir el-Bahri on the west side of the Nile, across from Luxor. It is one of the architectural marvels of our planet. After her death, her outraged son-in-law Thutmose III, whose rightful throne Hatshepsut had usurped, ordered her name removed from memory. Fortunately, he did not succeed.

CHAPTER FOURTEEN
Myths and Tales

Religion dominated life in Egypt even more than it did in Mesopotamia. That stemmed from the Egyptian belief in a possibly *happy afterlife, which had to be earned*. Egyptian pharaohs spent a great deal of the national wealth preparing for a luxurious after-death future, which they felt they had already earned. Far too many of those kings considered themselves divine.

One scholarly source suggests that Egypt had only 440 gods and goddesses. One equally reliable source assures us that Egypt never had more than 2,000 divinities. Perhaps the first believed the smaller number to be correct for a particular time period he had in mind, and the second thought the larger figure was correct for Egypt over the long-haul of about 5,000 years. However, one story has it that a pharaoh decided to build a memorial in which each of the deities of Egypt would have its own space, and that took 3,000 rooms.

In Egypt, as in Mesopotamia, there was a religious culture that shifted significantly over the centuries. Accordingly, gods and goddesses changed their names, their functions, and their symbolic representations. Some disappeared, some were resurrected, and some were combined. There were several Egyptian deities whose characteristics remained relatively stable over time, and some who changed, but in one way or another remained significant.

Egyptian mythology was well-endowed with creation stories. In one early version of their union, the Goddess of the Sky, *NUT*, and the earth-god *GEB* were the first divine lovers. At dawn, their first child, the sun, was born. At dusk, their second child, the moon, was born.

The Egyptians, like the Sumerians, assigned divinity to natural phenomena such as the sun, the moon, the five visibly-moving planets, and the Nile. But they also developed a more sophisticated theology, which included a *self-created* God of the Air, *AMON* (or *AMUN*). His worship was dominant in Upper Egypt, in the south, until the successful rebellion against the rule of the Hyksos.

**Figure 25: God of the Air, AMON,
with feathered headdress**

After that, Amon soon became a popular deity for the entire land, and was hailed as the King of the Gods. In language that resembles Mesopotamian praise for deities and divine kings, Amon became a god who stood for social justice—defending the weak and protecting the poor. As his popularity spread across Egypt, the wealth and power of Amon priests grew steadily.

At one point, the temples of Amon owned 60 towns outright with all their supporting land and industries, 10% of all the rest of Egypt's agricultural land, and 400,000 animals.

They also had 90,000 serfs and slaves to work their fields. The priests of Amon in effect controlled a sizeable portion of the national economy, and this often led the priests and pharaohs to play deadly games with each other.

The Sun God *RA*, also written as *RE*, was involved in several of Egypt's many creation stories. One said that Ra was the creative father who brought forth all living things *spontaneously*—all races of people and all plants and animals were created at once. Then they spread over the face of the earth.

There is no mention of Ra doing this in a certain number of days, although the popular Egyptian number was *seven*. As mentioned earlier, the Egyptians knew the same seven heavenly bodies known to the Sumerians.

Figure 26: The Sun God RA in the solar boat that carried him across the skies[60]

Ra created the first people, and they were both flawless and happy. However, as in Sumerian mythology, they were given the gift of *free will*. Over time, they slipped into imperfection, from their free-will transgressions. So, on his own initiative, Ra destroyed almost all people, not with a great flood, but with a great *drought* that he, the scorching sun, created. The few survivors were saved by a timely flood of the Nile. Thereafter, they had to plow the fields, irrigate them, and work hard forever.

Eventually, Amon and Ra were combined and worshipped for centuries as *AMON-RA*. In Egypt, Amon, God of the Air, was essentially a hidden god; Ra, God of the Sun, was magnificently visible every day.

PTAH, God of the Earth, developed after the earlier earth-god, *GEB*. In another creation story, it was Ptah who caused the Primordial Hill to rise up from out of Primordial Waters. Having willed creation in his heart, Ptah created the world by *naming the names*. He said "light," and there was light; he said "fresh water," and there was fresh water. Appropriately, Ptah was worshipped by Egypt's many artisans.

Figure 27: PTAH, God of the Earth

At the moment that land appeared out of the deep, so did a beautiful new winged goddess, *MA'AT*. She symbolized all that was noble and necessary for a truly superior civilization: justice, truth, order, and righteousness.

Figure 28: The Goddess MA'AT

Over time, Ma'at came to stand not only for a goddess with that name and those values, but also for the *cosmic order* that the pharaoh should maintain throughout his kingdom.

In this sense, Ma'at provided the pharaoh instruction on how to rule. He could resolve any crisis if he approached it with Ma'at and her principles of justice, truth, order, and righteousness. Righteousness meant *morality*, as Egypt's civilization defined it; and permitting *injustice* was seen as the worst possible kind of immoral behavior.

Over time, Ma'at became a kind of universal spiritual guide for all Egyptians—nobles, commoners, and slaves. It was a set of underlying principles of goodness by which each person measured his or her own life.

Any personal misdeeds accumulated in the human heart. When you died, your heart was weighed on a double-sided scale against the single feather that Ma'at wore in her hair. If the misdeeds in your heart outweighed Ma'at's feather, then your heart was tossed to a combination crocodile-hippopotamus god named *AMMIT*, who promptly ate it. And that was the end of your spiritual journey.

Eventually, Ptah, whose initial actions fostered Ma'at, was combined with Amon-Ra. That gave Egypt a holy trinity: *AMON-RA-PTAH*, God of Air, Sun, and Earth. In that unified form, Amon-Ra-Ptah became the Supreme Deity of Egypt.

Some ancient Egyptian writers declared that all creation stories were childish nonsense. They also argued that all human beings had evolved from brutes that once walked on all fours but had no speech. Most tellingly, those brutes were barbarian, because they had no *art*. These unknown authors may have been educated scribes who were not priests.

Incidentally, similar expressions of doubt were found on early clay tablets in Sumeria. Thoughtful doubt is common to human experience, so most likely these particular views were independently derived. Of course, we will never know which ideas accompanied the movement of people and goods between the two civilizations.

In spite of the occasional doubter, several of Egypt's gods and goddesses were worshipped widely. Of these, *ISIS* was preeminent. Isis comes closest to those mysterious mother goddesses of the very distant past. Worshipped as the ideal mother, she was the most enduring of the Egyptian deities. She would even be known, and worshipped, in far-flung areas under Greek and Roman rule, many centuries after her first temples appeared in Egypt.

**Figure 29: ISIS, the Great Mother,
with a throne headdress**

Isis was given credit for many of the great cultural inventions, including agriculture, literature and art. Egyptian women appreciated Isis as the protector of children.

To understand the true position of Isis, we have to introduce a particularly important male divinity, *OSIRIS*, the God of the Nile. Osiris was both brother and husband to Isis, a not-uncommon set of relationships in early mythology, generally.

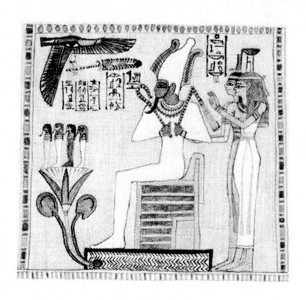

Figure 30: OSIRIS, God of the Nile, with attendants

Osiris is shown as having a green skin, probably meant to be the color of the Nile with its usual algae content. Because the Nile flooded and receded annually, Egyptian mythology introduced the idea that Osiris was killed every year by his jealous brother, *SETH*, the demon god of the desert. Seth could bring drought, desiccation and death. His hot breath could shrivel a grain crop overnight.

In the course of the year, Osiris and the Nile would be resurrected, all through the love of his wife, Isis. As in the Inanna and Dumuzi (Tammuz) stories from Sumeria, it was only love that could work the miracle of resurrection, and Egyptian women were devoted to Isis for her example of faithful, romantic love.

Isis and Osiris had a son, *HORUS*. Egyptian mythology said that Horus was born in a stable. His mother, Isis, was often depicted in paintings and bas-relief sculpture, as nursing Horus in a stable among the animals. Early Christians in Egypt, noting the similarity to the story of Mary and Jesus, would worship a carving or painting of Isis and Horus.

Like most gods in Egypt, Horus had an animal-spirit counterpart, the falcon. In the form of a falcon, Horus gradually became one of Egypt's most important gods. He was known as *The King of Egypt,* and this made it rather convenient for pharaohs who coveted a declaration of divinity by the high priests. As in Sumeria, that desire was a bargaining tool for the priests, who wanted the ruler to stay away from the temple treasury.

At the Egyptian Museum in Cairo, there is a particularly beautiful statue of the great king Khafre seated on his throne. One of the finest examples of Egyptian sculpture, it is made of polished diorite, a stone as hard as many gemstones. The statue was found buried under the floor of Khafre's temple at Memphis, the oldest of Egypt's cities, and the one that commanded the approaches to the delta of the Nile. Today Khafre's statue is one of the Egyptian Museum's main attractions.

Figure 31: Khafre and Horus

Notice how the Falcon God, Horus, envelopes Khafre's head. Horus was a part of Khafre's being! Khafre began his long rule around 2520 BCE, as the fourth king of the Fourth Dynasty. That is a little before the first Sumerian king was declared to be divine. Khafre may look a bit familiar—his face is on the Sphinx, as well.

One other Egyptian divinity well worth remembering is the Goddess *HATHOR*—Goddess of Joy, Love, and Music. She also helped women at childbirth. Because one of her representations was as a giant milk-giving cow, Hathor was also believed to help children. Egyptian artists usually painted Hathor as a lovely young woman, perhaps because one of her main jobs was to be the first one to greet you when you entered the afterlife.

Figure 32: HATHOR Greeting Thutmose I

In this bas-relief, Hathor is shown greeting Pharaoh Thutmose I on his arrival in the Afterlife.[61] From the looks of things, Hathor is giving Thutmose high and low fives, which was not a bad way to begin life on the Other Side.

In spite of some occasional rewards from a successful war, the Pharaohs always wanted taxes, and they had the enforcers to extract payment in kind from the fellahin. To put it mildly, it was hard for Egyptian peasants to keep body and soul together, after taxes. But they did believe they had a soul, as did all Egyptians. For them, the soul had three parts: The Akh, the Ka, and the Ba. Although ideas about these three changed somewhat over time, there were certain principal notions about them.

The Akh was a beautiful concept. When your body died, your Akh became a new star, with a polar orbit through the sky. The Ka was more of a problem—it was your 'spirit body double,' which unfortunately had all the daily needs of your body. The Ba was something like a hummingbird with your head on it. It flitted around your body as a winged conscience. After your death, it joined the Ka in making a pitch on your behalf to Osiris, so Osiris would let you be ferried across the River of the Dead to the happy Field of Food.

The particular role of the Ba was to tell Osiris about all the sins that you had *not* committed. The Egyptian Book of the Dead lists 42 things that *"I Have Not Done"* to be proclaimed by the Ba. Each is addressed to a different deity.

Many Egyptians memorized all 42 so their Ba would not forget. Here the opening lines of one of many versions of the Ba's formal *"Negative Confession"* to the court of OSIRIS, but without the long salute to the god which preceded each line:

> *"I have not committed crimes against people,*
> *I have not mistreated cattle,*
> *I have not sinned in the Place of Truth.*[62]
> *I have not known what should not be known,*
> *I have not done any harm..."*

(There may have been times when it was difficult for Osiris to keep a straight face.)

All in all, in spite of the need and hope for Ma'at, the Egyptians were very much aware of the human proclivity for sin. They sought a forgiving grace from their gods and goddesses.

After 1,000 years or so, Osiris was given an expanded role, and I'm not certain it was a promotion. He became overlord of the Egyptian *afterworld*. His new job was to decide on the fate of the recently deceased who had already been examined by a panel of 14 pure judges, and whose heart had passed the Ma'at feather test. Osiris wasn't easy to satisfy, but his final approval was necessary before a deceased person was permitted to cross the River of the Dead into the Egyptian version of heaven.

As with most heavens, it was hard to reach. The Egyptian heaven was called the *Field of Food*, and that says much about its attraction for an ordinary Egyptian citizen. Peasants who reached the field of food still had to work, but there was no possibility of their greatest fear—crop failure.

Incidentally, the Egyptian River of the Dead is generally credited as the basis for the Greeks' idea of the River Styx. Both the Egyptians and the Greeks got across those rivers with the aid of a special ferryman.

We are familiar with the pyramids and the elaborate tombs for the nobility and the wealthy in Egypt. For the poor, burial in the desert to the west of the Nile was the best they could hope for. The sun set in the west, so that was the direction for burial of the common man. But that may not have been as bad as it sounds.

A few years ago in Great Britain, a grave site was uncovered for a burial that took place around 700 CE. The body had been placed about four feet from the surface. In that damp climate, the buried man had almost totally disintegrated. All that was left in fair condition was one tooth! The recently recovered remains of an Egyptian peasant buried about 3200 BCE was found to the west of the Nile. It had been covered with only four feet of sand in the desert, but it was as nicely preserved as most upper-class mummies!

There is a sculpture that suggests a late influence of Greek culture on Egypt. It dates to about 350 BCE, and may have been done by a Greek living in Egypt. This sculpture is famous for its soft modeling—the way that the planes of the form merge so gently.

In Egypt, the Cairo Museum had a seated Egyptian figure in a carved chair, but it was headless. The Brooklyn Museum, in greater New York City, had a beautiful sculptured Egyptian head, but no body. On the back of the head was the name of the Egyptian priest portrayed by the sculpture, *Wesirwir.* Some thought that Wesirwir was actually Osiris himself, given the green color of the sculpture.

Figure 33: The Head of Wesirwir

An Egyptologist determined that the two pieces were from the same sculpture, so the Egyptian government asked that the head be returned. The answer wasn't exactly "Fageddaboudit!" but the Brooklyn Museum did politely decline. However, the powers that be in Egypt graciously let the Brooklyn Museum display the two pieces together for one exhibition. It was a perfect fit.

CHAPTER FIFTEEN
Borrowing, Again

In order to comprehend the enormous time periods involved in regard to Egypt, we must know that its art had reached cultural high-points in four fields—architecture, sculpture, literature, and music—more than 250 years before Joseph and his family arrived in Egypt. By my reckoning, the family came in from a drought-stricken Canaan somewhere around 1670 BCE. Joseph had been traded into Egypt by his jealous brothers some 35 years earlier.

The Bible states that the Hebrews were in Egypt for a period of 430 years, beginning with Joseph's family and ending with the Exodus. That was more than enough time for profound cultural assimilation. It is not surprising that a significant part of the literature, concepts, and cultural practices of the Jews can be traced back to their experience in the land of the pharaohs. Some of the main borrowings are enumerated below.

We need to note again that over some 2,000 years, Sumerian and Egyptian creation stories had a great deal in common. For example, both had myths that suggested the presence of deep water before there was anything else. Creation was accomplished in both sets of stories by divine command through *naming the names*, and by actually *molding and fashioning the materials of creation*. It is certainly not surprising that the Hebrew authors of the stories of creation in *Genesis* used the same two themes. After all, their ancestors had lived in both Mesopotamia and Egypt for very long periods of time.

1.   *Food avoidances.* We should know that pork was commonly eaten in northern Egypt around the great delta of the Nile, where there were many non-Egyptian outsiders living. That was not the case in southern Egypt, which was centered on the city of Thebes, which we know today as Luxor. However, around 3200 BCE, southern Egypt conquered northern Egypt, and so pork avoidance became more widespread in the north.

Eating pork was somehow associated with the evil god Seth of the desert. Wild pigs on the fringes of the narrow cultivated areas were a threat to the crops and the survival of farmers in those areas. But eventually, only Egyptian priests were forbidden to eat pork, along with shellfish. In those later times, some temples even raised pigs for profit on their large landholdings.

Also, as garbage scavengers, pigs were quite useful in helping to keep the rat population under control. The temple priests were very much interested in that, because the temples were major owners of cultivated land, and rats feasted on crops at night.

It is interesting that in the Old Testament book of *Leviticus*, which outlines in detail the complicated food avoidances and dietary laws to be observed, the Hebrew people are called upon to make their entire nation *"a holy priesthood."* Food avoidances that were practiced only by Egyptian priests not long before were now required of all Jews.

2. *Circumcision.* This practice also began with the temple priesthood in ancient Egypt. And, circumcision is a very early topic in the Old Testament. In fact, it appears in *Genesis* 17 as a part of the covenant Abraham established with God on behalf of the Jewish people. And we need to remember that, long before that text was written, Abraham went to live in Egypt when a drought kept him from settling his family in Canaan after they had left Haran in southeastern Turkey.

The oldest documentary evidence for circumcision of any form comes from ancient Egypt, centuries before Abraham's father decided that it was time for the family to leave Ur, in Sumeria. Young novitiates for the Egyptian priesthood were circumcised individually, or in groups of up to 200 at a time, as a health requirement. Egyptian artists who decorated tombs put that scene on the walls in full view.

The Greek historian Herodotus wrote, after a visit to Egypt around 450 BCE: *"The priests are all circumcised, choosing to be healthy, rather than handsome."* To us, that is a curious statement, but the Greeks believed that circumcision detracted from the beauty of the male body. Perhaps more important was their view that a male was never really naked if his penis still had its foreskin.

As a result, most of the people conquered by Alexander the Great never adopted the practice of circumcision, or if they had adopted it earlier, they soon gave it up. The Jews came to see Greek culture as a special threat to their own way of life, so they held on—you might say, *religiously*—to the practice of circumcision. Certainly, it was a notable way to proclaim their separateness from the Hellenistic world.

3. *Baptism.* Ritual baptism was first practiced in ancient Egypt, long before the Jews arrived by way of either Abraham or Joseph. Early Egyptian baptismal sites were hollowed-out stone basins in front of the

temples of the sun god, Ra, whose main temple was at Heliopolis, in northern Egypt. Ra was particularly associated with the sun at high noon.

Some 500 years or so before the Jews came into Egypt, Ra had been united with a god from southern Egypt, *AMON* (AMUN). Amon was the god of the wind and a creator god who upheld justice and righteousness. By the time the Hebrews were enslaved, *AMON-RA* had evolved as the all-important sun god. Amon-Ra was the dominant Egyptian deity for most of the time the Jews were in Egypt, and that was a time when Egyptians worshipped at least 600 deities.

Of all the lands around the Mediterranean, Egypt was regarded as having reached the highest levels of cultural development. It attracted people from all over the known world. Because an outsider would not be accepted into Egyptian society until he or she had fully adopted Egyptian cultural practices, it is not surprising that foreign migrants to Egypt often wanted permission to worship Egyptian gods and goddesses. They could do so only after a period of priestly instruction that culminated in an immersion baptism at high noon. The baptism took place in a hollowed out stone near a sun temple.

The person being baptized was lifted straight out of the water by a temple priest, who held on to the convert's head until the eyes of that newly baptized person looked directly at the sun, for an instant. It was meant to be a transfixing experience, and it probably was. Just observing it, as the Jews could have done many times, must have led to a thoughtful consideration of baptism as a purifying ritual.

We don't know exactly when the Jews finally adopted baptism, but when they did, they used the same wording for it as did the Egyptian hieroglyphics for baptism: *the waters of purification*. A proselyte, or convert, to Judaism was considered unclean until after the baptismal ritual, called *mikvah*. Mikvah (or mikveh) called for full immersion in *the living waters*, a term also borrowed from the Egyptians. After baptism, regardless of age, the convert to Judaism was said to be *a child just born*.

Because of the common cosmology/theology featuring the sun, moon and five planets, seven was a special number for the Egyptians, as it had first been for the Sumerians. It also became a special number for the Jews, as we know from many passages in the Old Testament. Jewish priests baptized all male proselytes entering Judaism exactly seven days after their circumcision.

The Hebrew Torah—those first five books of the Old Testament—suggested many ways in which a person might become unclean. For example, if you touched a corpse you were ritually unclean; if you ate any part of an unclean animal, you were unclean. In order to become clean again, you had to go through the mikvah ritual. In Orthodox Judaism, women were and still are considered unclean after giving birth, and during and after their menstrual cycle until purified or *made clean* by mikvah. Orthodox Jewish women were, and are today, the primary users of the mikvah ritual.

The special baptismal structure used in Jewish baptism is also called a *mikvah*. Pictures of very old mikvahs in Israel look something like those earlier Egyptian baptismal sites—basins cut out of stone.

The baptism of an infant suggests that baptism is the beginning, not the end, of that person's faith journey. In Egypt, *The Book of the Dead* dealt with the obligations of preparing the soul for its afterlife. (It was also titled *The Book of Going Forth by Day.*) Written near the time the Jews left Egypt, it contained a treatise on the baptism of newborn children as a way to insure that children's souls were initiated in the right manner.

4. *Proverbs.* To discuss proverbs properly requires that we also include some relevant material from Sumeria, as well as Egypt. Proverbs were very important to both of these early civilizations, for the same reason. Like epic poems, folk wisdom reminded you of your cultural identity.

Like the Sumerians, the Egyptians had a very large collection of proverbs, and they provided much material for the biblical book of *Proverbs*. These aphorisms had been an oral tradition for many centuries, but Egyptian scribes began writing their proverbs down about 2400 BCE. That practice continued on to the end of the Egyptian dynasties, when the Roman conquest was complete.

While the Hebrew people were in captivity in Egypt, a court counselor to Ramses II selected 610 of these proverbs, which he put into one text. His name was Amenemopet, (or, *'Amen-em-Opet,'* in some translations), and he described his work as *"advice from a father to his son."* Scribes made many copies of Amenemopet's book over the centuries, as they did with nine other books of Egyptian proverbs that ranged in time of composition from 2600 BCE all the way down to just 30 years before Jesus' arrival on the scene.

Here are a few samples of Amenemopet's advice to his son:

> *Don't be greedy for a cubit of land, and don't trespass on the boundaries of the widow.*
> *Plow the fields to meet your own needs, and make your bread from your own threshing floor. A bushel which God gives you is better than five thousand gained by transgression.*
> *Poverty in the hand of God is better than riches in the storehouse, and a crust of bread, when*

your heart it joyous, is better than riches in
unhappiness.[63]

After reading proverb collections in both areas, the not-so-startling deduction is that Mesopotamia and Egypt must have shared a great many proverbs with each other and with everybody else in their parts of the world.

Amenemopet divided his book into 30 chapters. The Old Testament book of *Proverbs* 22:20-21 reads: *"Have I not written for you thirty sayings of admonition and knowledge, to show you what is right and true…"* Those who wrote down *Proverbs* seem to have borrowed 16 of them from Amenemopet, expressing nearly the same thoughts, but not identical renditions.

Here is an example of a fairly typical Egyptian proverb and a Biblical proverb covering the same topic: the need to respect the boundaries and markers of private property. The Egyptian proverb is very clear and quite specific:

"Do not carry off the landmark at the boundar-
ies of the arable land, nor disturb the position
of the measuring cord."

In the King James Version of the Bible, *Proverbs* 22:28, the writer uses a similar image:

> *"Remove not the ancient landmarks which your fathers have set."*

The King James version includes a patriarchal twist that wasn't in the Egyptian original. The New Revised Standard Version of the Bible does change *"fathers"* to *"ancestors,"* but it still pales alongside the Egyptian original.

5. *Amen.* That Egyptian collector of proverbs, Amenemopet, was either too busy or too modest to sign his long full name every time he completed a set of proverbs, so he just put in the abbreviation for his name, *Amen.* This was during the time the Jews were in Egypt. Within a century or so after Amenemopet's death, his signature *Amen* had understandably evolved to mean *truly* or *certainly.* It may have been one of hundreds of loan words that were added to Hebrew.

Amen is only used 30 times in the Old Testament, whose first writings were about 600 years after the Exodus from Egypt. When Amen was used, it meant the same as it did to the later Egyptians reading their proverbs: *truly, verily, so be it.*

However, Jesus, who spent some early time in Egypt, used *Amen* some 99 times in the New Testament. There are 30 additional *Amens* in the New Testament, for a total of 129. Biblical dictionaries most often give its meaning as *truly* or *verily.*

Even so, Biblical scholars, Jewish and Christian, have gone to great lengths to dig up root words in Hebrew as the possible basis for *Amen.* They are not particularly convincing. *Amen* is simply an interesting example of a word taking on a new and meaningful role, quite different from its original one.

6. *The eternal soul.* As you might guess, the idea of the soul has a long and multi-layered history. The ancient Sumerians believed in a future life, but one in which the dead all went to a dismal underworld called *Kur.* The underworld took on different names with conquests of the Sumerian region.

Following that lead, early Hebrew writings in the Old Testament suggested something quite similarly depressing—a dark pit of a netherworld, an abyss called *Sheol.* As *Deuteronomy* and *Job* made clear, that was the destination of every dead person, with no distinction between the wicked and the righteous. There was no mention in the early texts of an immortal soul, but there is in the book of *Daniel,* added to the Old Testament about 165 BCE. The book of Daniel was the last entry into the Old Testament.

After his visit to Egypt in the fifth century before Christ, Herodotus wrote that the Egyptians were first to develop the idea of an immortal soul that might live on after the death of the body. And, he acknowledged that the Greeks borrowed the notion of an immortal soul from the Egyptians. (Incidentally, the Greek afterworld was called *Hades*.)

Most of us find Egypt's pyramids intriguing. In Sumeria, the ziggurats played a major role in the religious life of the people; in Egypt, the pyramids did not. For the most part, they were dramatically large, expensive burial sites for kings with huge egos, and equally large expectations for the afterlife.

When Herodotus visited Giza, he arrived more than 2,000 years after the pyramids were constructed. Herodotus believed some then-current but incorrect theories about the building of the pyramids. Priests told him that 100,000 slaves had done the work. Recent translations of writings by the men in charge of the pyramid-building projects tell a very different story.

According to these writings, off-season farmers were organized in teams ranging in size from 20 to 35 men, and each team had its own supply of blocks and tackle, pulleys, and sleds. Each group of workers had its own foreman, and each group was given specific assignments. Organizationally, it was a much more impressive undertaking than conscripting 100,000 slaves.

The engineers built hard-surfaced roads from the Nile and from the local quarry to the construction sites, that were paved with the same stone used in the pyramids. Herodotus was almost as impressed by the roads as he was by the Great Pyramid! However, 300 years later, when the Greeks listed the Seven Wonders of the World, they didn't mention the roads, but they did include the Great Pyramid.

Another one of the ancient Seven Wonders was the Lighthouse at Pharos, built on a little island near the harbor at Alexandria at the north end of the Nile delta. The lighthouse must have been impressive—towering some 500 feet—and that made it even higher than the Great Pyramid in its prime. The Greek committee that chose the Seven Wonders may have been influenced by the fact that it was the work of a Greek architect who lived in Alexandria.[64] They passed over the Sphinx, which had already deteriorated seriously over the 2,000 years since it had been constructed.

In Egypt, the oldest pyramids date to around 2600 BCE, and they were built with the idea of supplying the after-life needs of the eternal soul. But, there were horizontal tombs built centuries before the pyramids, and they had the same purpose. The idea of an immortal soul developed in Egypt long before either Abraham or Joseph came onto the scene. (Incidentally, the Step Pyramid at Saqqara is older than the first ziggurat in Sumeria, and their purposes were widely different.)

The Jews had been thoroughly exposed to Greek culture by the time the Biblical book of *Daniel* was written, and that must also have contributed in some way to their long-term views as to an immortal soul. However, my guess is that the major impact was from another source—from their Babylonian captivity. And, of course, that is what the book of *Daniel* is about.

Israel's Pharisees developed as a powerful group after their experience in the Captivity, and they picked up and championed the notion of the eternal soul from their exposure to Zoroastrianism. (Incidentally, Zoroastrians believe that the Pharisees got their name from being those who had learned the Persian language, Farsi, and the culture that accompanied it.)

7. *A loving god as a role model.* Over time, both Sumerian and Egyptian worship turned into a devotional process, in which one's character and behavior was shaped by the god you worshipped.

After the Middle Kingdom ended about 1670 BCE, which was about the time Joseph's family arrived in Egypt, the Egyptian gods were thought to be more interested in good character and love for your fellow man. Listen to these proverbs recorded by Egyptian scribes at that time:

The character of one who is upright in heart is more acceptable to the gods than is the sacrifice of an ox by an evildoer.

A good character is a remembrance: give the love of yourself to the whole world. (In other words, as the Bible teaches, *love your neighbor as yourself.*)

8. *Monotheism.* The most controversial subject in this short list, and the most meaningful, has to do with the rise of monotheism in the faith of the Hebrew people. Something happened while the Hebrews were in Egypt that could not have failed to attract their attention, and it may have captured their spiritual core. The event occurred after 1379 BCE, when a new pharaoh was appointed—Amonhotep IV.

Because he was only eight years old at the time, he was made co-regent with his father until his father died, when Amonhotep was 20. He had had 12 years to observe and think about the role of religion in his country. After all, he had been named for the god AMON, and was following kings who thought they were gods themselves.

The young pharaoh could hardly help noticing the corruption of the priests, who were selling charms and practicing magic. They were constantly involved in the worst of royal court politics, including an occasional assassination. Amonhotep went to the temple at Karnak, and the temple courtesans, who were supposed to serve all the men who came to worship, had just become prostitutes for the priests.

He noted that the priests consumed the food given in worship, and nothing was given to the poor. The temples were indecently wealthy, and yet always wanted more. Amonhotep was disgusted, as the Hebrew slaves must have been as well.

When Amonhotep did become pharaoh on his own at the age of 20, he promptly blew Egypt's religious life apart. He decreed that there are not 440 gods—not even 10 gods—there is only one god, and his name is *ATEN*. He is the Lord of Heaven, but Aten belongs to all nations, not just Egypt. The solar disc was used as a symbol for Aten because God reaches down, like the sun, to bring life. But Aten is not the sun—Aten is everything. Aten (also translated as Aton) is the One True God, who lives on truth. The young pharaoh's profound spiritual experience led him to change his name to *AKHENATEN*, which means *May it please Aten*. He chose a beautiful young woman, Nefertiti, as his wife.

Figure 34: Akhenaten

Figure 35: Nefertiti

Akhenaten ordered all the old temples closed, putting thousands of furious priests and others employed in the temples out of work. The common people—uneducated and poorly informed—were disturbed because their old familiar gods and goddesses were gone. Everyone in Egypt had to have been talking about these revolutionary changes, including the enslaved Hebrews.

With his pacifist views, Akhenaten had very little use for the army, and its officers were just as unhappy as the priests. Somehow, Akhenaten managed to survive and rule for nine years before his death in 1363 BCE. Most Egyptologists assume Akhenaten was assassinated.

Some say that Nefertiti managed to rule for the next three years, but shortly after that, when King Tut came onto the throne, all signs of their rule were demolished and removed from public view. Whenever Egyptian historians had to refer to Akhenaten, they were required to call him *The Great Criminal*.

Television's *Discovery* and *History* channels made quite a stir over the re-opening of an old tomb that was first found in 1908. A few years ago, in looking at some early photographs of the mummies inside, an archaeologist realized that the profile of one looked very much like the famous sculptured bust of Nefertiti. There is substantial supporting evidence that it really is her mummified body, so at long last her burial site seems to have been determined.

When Akhenaten's successor, King Tut, became the new pharaoh, he was only nine years old. From the beginning, Tut was a pawn of the priests who led the worship of the old god, *AMON*. Everything was quickly restored to the old ways of doing business.

Fortunately, and largely accidentally, a fair amount of material from Akhenaten's reign was preserved. This is particularly so in regard to his diplomatic exchanges with areas of Mesopotamian culture recorded on clay tablets. They were found in a mound called Tel Amarna, along with the remains of Akhenaten's new city, Akhetaten, intended to be the new spiritual center of Egypt.

One special find in Amarna was the remains of the city's artist workshops. From the artifacts found, we know that both painting and sculpture flourished during Akhenaten's brief reign. Visual art was the most relaxed and natural at any time in Egypt's history. An unfinished sculpture of Nefertiti confirms and demonstrates the changes that were underway.

Figure 36: Unfinished bust of Nefertiti found at Tel Amarna

Even the dress required in court went from formal costume to informal clothing. Literature changed from antiquated scholarly language to writing in the common speech of the Egyptian people—and that would have been the language understood by most of the Hebrew slaves after more than 300 years in Egypt.

There is a moving hymn written by Akhenaten about 1340 BCE called *"Hymn to the Aten."* This is one of the finest of all the literary works produced in Egypt, and it would not look out of place if it were in the Bible. In fact, some of its lines *do* appear in the Bible. Here are a few lines adapted from this much longer, masterful work:

"How manifold are your works!
So many that some are even hidden from us.
O only God, whose powers no other possesses,
You created the earth according to your heart,
While you were alone:
All people, all cattle large and small,
All that are on the earth,
All that go about on their feet,
All that are on high, flying with their wings!
You created all the foreign countries,
And the land of Egypt.
You set all persons into their places,
And you supply their necessities.

How excellent are your designs,
O Lord of eternity.
You are in my heart.
There is no other.
Men live through you
While their eyes are on your beauty!
You did establish the world."[65]

Some biblical scholars feel the need to write off this part of the Jews' experience in Egypt, supposedly because it took place several hundred years before the Old Testament was written and compiled. But collective memories are mysterious, selective things.

As we have seen from the Hebrew people's much earlier experience in Sumeria, many ideas and beliefs and even texts were borrowed and then used in the Old Testament. It did not reduce their meaning to be borrowed, and they were often enhanced with a new devotion, a new spirit. It would seem that this form of evolution is the way God works in the spiritual world.

As a postscript to this chapter, I should mention two interesting Jewish writers who wrote about the impact of Egypt on the Hebrews and their religion. One was Abraham Shalom Yahuda, a linguist, author and collector of rare documents in the late 19th Century and first half of the 20th Century. He published his first book, _Arab Antiquities_, at the age of 15 in

1895. Yahuda also became known later on for his outspoken rebuke of Zionist policies.

The book by Yahuda that most interests us, in terms of the subjects under consideration, was titled _The Accuracy of the Bible_, which was published in 1934. It was a time when some historians were arguing that there had been no long stay in Egypt, and consequently, no Exodus. Their reasoning was based primarily on the fact that seemingly reliable Egyptian historians of the day never even mentioned the momentous events that are highlighted in the Bible.

Yahuda's intensive study of the Egyptian language convinced him that the Hebrew people had indeed spent a long time in Egypt. And yes, he believed that the Hebrew people left Egypt in an exodus to become the people of Israel. Yahuda pointed out that there are thousands of Egyptian loan words in the Torah. Yahuda noted that there are four Egyptian loan words in just the first sentence of the Hebrew account of Moses' birth. You have to live in the midst of another language for many years for your language to absorb so much of it.

The other Jewish scholar who had interesting things to say about the Egyptian impact on the Hebrew people was Sigmund Freud. In his day, Freud was one of the world's most outspoken atheists. His last book, _Moses and Monotheism_, was widely criticized as an attempt to psychoanalyze an entire people, but it was more than that.

Freud argued that Moses, who had an Egyptian name, was an Egyptian priest, not a fellow Hebrew. He noted that the mythology of any group requires its savior to be one of the group. Accordingly, Sargon 1's birth story, already more than 1,000 years old, was borrowed and adapted for the birth of Moses. For the Jews, Moses became a Jew with an Egyptian name. Moses led the Jews to Canaan because, while they were enslaved in Egypt, they had accepted Akhenaten's compelling call for belief in the One True God. Moses, Freud argued, was a priest of that new belief.

According to Freud, Akhenaten was soon gone from the earthly stage, but the captive Hebrews accepted and kept alive the core of Akhenaten's message. By focusing on the fact that they alone were the followers of the One True God, a concept that fit well with the spiritual wisdom of the ideas and stories they carried down from Mesopotamia, they founded a new religion. They were led from Egypt by Moses. Freud's arguments are reasonably credible in this first part of his book.

However, in the latter part of _Moses and Monotheism_, Freud claims that dissent among the Hebrews led to the murder of Moses, and that the Jews still exhibited a longstanding guilt complex stemming from that act against their deliverer. Most people of the 1930s who heard about the book were not inclined to read it, as criticism focused on that one outrageous part of an otherwise interesting text.

Once Freud was associated with this national guilt complex theory, word was out that he had gone balmy. However, there were informed scholars who believed him to be right in his basic argument: Moses was an Egyptian who led the enslaved Hebrews out of Egypt—the Jews being the one group that had found truth in Akhenaten's powerful message.

One of the intriguing bits of history is that Abraham Shalom Yahuda went to Sigmund Freud and tried to talk him out of publishing _Moses and Monotheism_. British playwright Terry Johnson wrote a play, _Hysteria_, which is mostly about an intriguing meeting between Freud, one of Freud's patients, and Salvador Dali. Abraham Yahuda is also a character in the play, and yes, he tries to talk Freud out of publishing _Moses and Monotheism_.

Freud's book can still be found in stores, and is even available in full, online. Productions of _Hysteria_ are occasionally produced in various parts of the U.S. There were recent productions on Cape Cod and in St. Petersburg, Florida. The complete title of Terry Johnson's play is _"Hysteria: Or Fragments of an Analysis of an Obsessional Neurosis."_

CHAPTER SIXTEEN
Getting Out and Getting There

*E*xodus 1:13-14 says: *"And the Egyptians made the children of Israel to serve with vigor, and they made their lives bitter with hard bondage in mortar and brick."* The Bible names the two *warehouse cities* the enslaved Hebrews were building: Rameses and Pithom. They were to be supply depots for Rameses II, the last of the great Egyptian pharaohs. He ruled from 1279 BCE to 1213 BCE.

Rameses II had re-conquered much of Canaan, and brought back many more slaves. This would help account for the large number who took part in the Exodus. According to the biblical texts, there were 600,000 men, besides children, plus a mixed crowd of other folks who went along just to get out of Egypt. They don't mention the number of women, suggesting that by the time the story of the Exodus was written down, Hebrew society was so patriarchal that women weren't particularly noticed, unless they misbehaved or saved a great number of its men.

Rameses II was a phenomenal builder, constructing more than half of all surviving structures built by the pharaohs, and leaving even more built artifacts than the great queen-king, Hatshepsut. The Hebrew people suffered under this self-idolized god-king.

You remember the story: Moses fled for his life to the Midianites after killing a cruel Egyptian slave master. The Midianites were one of several Semitic tribes that traced their ancestry back to Abraham through one of the six seldom-mentioned sons of Abraham and Keturah. (Keturah became Abraham's wife after the death of Sarah.)

If Moses was an Egyptian, as the Egyptian historian Manetho believed, he could have gone to the Midianites with the blessing of their distant kin, the Hebrews.[66]Usually, relatives offered the best chance for sanctuary.

Moses was always interested in knowing God's name. The Midianites worshipped Ba'al and the Queen of Heaven, Ashtoreth, but they also had a god, *YAHU*, or *YAH*, suggesting a Mesopotamian connection. Moses went back to Egypt, after the voice from the burning bush reminded him of the suffering of the Hebrew people.

In spite of the powerful acts of Moses and his brother Aaron, Rameses was reluctant to give up the slaves who were working on his two new cities. As the story goes, God sent plagues to change Rameses' mind. The Nile turned to blood, killing all the fish; then there were frogs, gnats, flies, death of all the animals from a sudden disease, an outbreak of boils, a terrible hail storm, swarms of locusts, three days of darkness, and finally the clincher, the death of all first-born children, but with the homes of obedient Hebrews *passed over*.

About those plagues: Egypt has the longest recorded history of plagues of any country on earth. Over the course of that lengthy history, it has had a plague of some sort about once every 15 years, with some resembling the biblical plagues in one way or another. If the Hebrew people were in Egypt for 430 years, as the Bible says, then they would have experienced some 28 plagues while they were there. Locusts may have been the most common disorder, but a massive red algae bloom can kill the fish in the Nile, make the water both blood red and deadly to drink.

The biblical text itself suggests that a very long period of time was involved in the story. All the animals were killed in one plague, but then in the very next plague, all the animals broke out in boils. Following that, all the animals were killed by hail, and so on. Either the events took place over an extensive time period or an impressive amount of literary license was used in telling the story![67]

Reluctantly, Rameses told Moses to take the Hebrew people out of Egypt. Soon after they began to leave, Rameses changed his mind and sent his army to recapture them. The Egyptologist John Romer thinks the inspiration for the story of parting the Red Sea may have come from Babylonian mythology, in which the god Marduk cuts in half Tiamat, the goddess of salt water. That is not a particularly close mythological fit, but it is worth considering.

The story as told may have been about a real thing. The most likely escape route for the Hebrews would have taken them near the shallow Bitter Lakes, just north of the Red Sea. In the Bitter Lakes, a very strong prevailing wind can push the water back and dry the ground quickly. If the wind suddenly slackens, the water washes back over the area. *Exodus 14:21-22* gives a description somewhat similar to that.

The Hebrew people did get out of Egypt, somewhere around 1240 BCE. Almost all scholars think the number of people involved was greatly inflated in the biblical text. Neither Goshen, where the slaves were concentrated in Egypt, nor the wilderness of Sinai could possibly have supported such huge numbers—more than two million, with women and children included. It would take a lot more than quail and manna to feed that crowd for 40 years!

Of course, an exodus of anything approaching this scale would suggest that herds of cattle and sheep were taken along, but the wilderness wasn't noted for its grass supply.

The animals wouldn't have lasted long at any rate, with so many people to feed. Incidentally, that wilderness was named Sin—not suggesting an inappropriate act, but the name of the Babylonian moon god, *SIN*.

The footnotes in the *New Revised Standard* version of the Bible are unusually straightforward about it being impossible for that many people to sustain themselves in the wilderness. Of course, that is one of the reasons why most Christian fundamentalists do not use that version of the Bible! They prefer "God's own authorized version," the *King James*.

CHAPTER SEVENTEEN
About Canaan

After being led by Moses to the border of the hill country east of the Jordan River, the Hebrew people returned to Canaan. They had taken a circuitous route to Canaan, probably to avoid contact and conflict with a group of powerful newcomers, the Philistines.

As a cultural region, Canaan originally included parts of what are now Syria and Lebanon. A large part of the central hill country, where the Twelve Tribes would build their strength, came to be known over time as Israel. After the death of Solomon, the land called Israel split into Judah in the south, and a new Israel in the north. Parts of a central sub-region, Samaria, were in both Judah and Israel.

All of these areas were forested in pre-historic times. On the better soils there were oaks, and on the poorer soils, a pine forest. As these lands were cleared, a kind of

Mediterranean scrub forest took over and had to be kept in check if you wanted to plant crops. You can still see that scrub forest today in areas with steep slopes and poor soil.

Olive trees were planted in place of the oaks because the oil was so valuable. In place of the pines, one could develop vineyards. Both of these were long-term bets with no immediate return. On flatter areas, wheat and barley were grown. Animal herding was practiced on the rest of the land, even though its carrying capacity was low.

That central sub-region, Samaria (from whence came the Good Samaritan) was the least productive: more hills, rougher terrain, and less moisture. About the only advantage it did have was its strategic location in the center of things. The Samaritan people may have become a little tougher over time due to their harsh environment, and they were often harshly treated by outsiders, particularly the conquering Assyrians. The Samaritans' bad reputation with the Jews is a separate story, which comes later.

In the wilderness, milk and honey may have been the substance of Hebrew dreams, but their tastes soon changed. *Psalms* 104:15 says that God sent *"wine to gladden the heart of man, oil to make his face shine, and bread to strengthen his heart."* After the Hebrew people became accustomed to this more elegant diet, the phrase *curds and honey* became a symbol of poverty.

There are two things we need to consider about Canaan, generally. First, Canaan was largely a Mesopotamian culture area where the Jews lived before they went into Egypt. Also, they had been in Mesopotamia itself for some 300-plus years before they came to Canaan the first time. They were well exposed to the ideas and mythology of this Sumerian-based civilization. That exposure provided the grounding for their religion, which they would modify with the passage of time.

Second, the Hebrews' return to Canaan and their behavior there, as given in the Old Testament, is not a historically accurate portrayal. (And that is a very welcome understanding!) Incidentally, that history is the center of a very nasty fight going on today, with Jewish and Christian fundamentalists allied against modern Jewish archaeologists and historians in an ugly disregard by the fundamentalists for rigorous scholarship.

To begin with that first point: the captive Hebrews were back in the largely Mesopotamian culture they experienced for many years in the Sumerian city of Ur. Canaan's version of that culture had changed over time—over about 2,000 years, actually—and local Canaanite names and stories had been assigned to Mesopotamian gods and goddesses imported long ago. Nonetheless, many of the basic religious ideas of Mesopotamia were still present in Canaan.

Canaan's territory extended from Egypt to modern-day Turkey and included what we know today as Israel, Jordan,

Lebanon, and parts of Syria. The old cities of Ugarit and Ebla pretty much marked the northern end, and the southern boundary ran from about 30 miles south of the city of Gaza to the Dead Sea.

As agriculture developed and flourished in Mesopotamia, Canaan was one of the first areas to receive migrants who knew how to grow wheat and barley. The Canaanites built villages and adopted irrigation practices as those powerful innovations spread from the valleys of the Tigris and Euphrates. Towns and cities then became possible in Canaan as food surpluses became available and trade flourished. Ideas always flowed along with the trade.

As noted before, Jericho was one of the first towns, possibly *the* first town on the planet. Jericho developed sometime around 9,000 BCE—in other words, about 11,000 years ago. Beirut was one of the first true cities to develop outside Mesopotamia, and recent excavations suggest that it dates back to about 3,000 BCE—some 5,000 years ago.

Canaanite cities and towns were in constant jeopardy because Canaan was vulnerable to attack by armies from both Egypt and Mesopotamia. Canaan was the vulnerable passage-way between these two major centers of power. Although Egypt may have invaded more frequently, Canaan's basic culture remained thoroughly Mesopotamian, based on the ideas, values, knowledge and religion of ancient Sumeria. Most of Canaan's people had moved there from

Mesopotamia, as population pressures, invasion, and warfare dictated.

Recall that the best ideas of Sumerian religion—in particular, pursuing justice and righteousness—had developed by 2500 BCE. By the time of the return of the Hebrew people, around 430 BCE, Canaan had been a cultural outpost of Mesopotamian civilization for over 1,000 years, maintained by the Akkadians, then the Babylonians, the Assyrians, the Kassites, the Hittites and the Hurrians, and finally by the Chaldeans (the New Babylonians).

Canaan's revised Mesopotamian culture even penetrated Egypt's borders in a few small settlements, but was much more prevalent in the Delta of the Nile. There, Egypt permitted Canaanite people to come in large numbers to raise animals for consumption in Egyptian cities.

By the chronology that seems to work best from my readings, the Hebrews are well entrenched in Canaan by 1230 BCE, and possibly a decade before. Some Jewish scholars are now suggesting that the Exodus took place almost 200 years earlier, but that gets the Hebrew people out of Egypt even before Rameses II. As was noted earlier, the Hebrew slaves were building his two warehouse cities, Rameses and Pithom, so they could hardly have left before his rule.

When they do get in sight of Canaan after their exodus from Egypt, the Hebrew people are hungry for food, land, cities, and everything else! Moses reported that God said they would soon have a *"land of milk and honey."* God had also said, on Moses' tablets with the Ten Commandments, *"Thou shalt not kill!"* However, according to the biblical account, the Israelites were out willingly slaughtering men, women, and children (including infants) to take over Canaan quickly.

Fortunately, modern scholarship absolves the Israelites (and God) from the account In Joshua of that wholesale slaughter of the innocents in Canaan. A particularly fine book, <u>The Bible Unearthed</u>,[67] gives very sound archaeological evidence that the takeover by the Hebrews was a gradual infiltration process, after many years of living as shepherds in the dry hill country to the east of the Jordan Valley.

Academically respected archaeologists now agree also that Jericho was not destroyed by the Israelites, but by some other group of invaders who brought those walls tumbling down at least 200 years before the Hebrew people arrived in Canaan. Earlier earthquakes probably played a part, as well.

Incidentally, both of these findings by modern scholars are bitterly opposed by fundamentalist Jews and Christians who insist that the Bible is an unerring historical document as well as a spiritual one. They have raised a great deal of money and employed their own "archaeologists" who agree that every word, date, and event found in their version of the Bible is sacrosanct and infallible.

Now, back to Canaan in 1230 BCE. Because so many different peoples had entered Canaan over the centuries, there were 14 different languages spoken in that fairly small area. Most of those were Semitic, but there were also Indo-European languages, such as that of the Hittites, and some unclassifiable ones, such as the language spoken by the Hurrians. As you would expect, modern archaeologists find evidence of many cross-cultural influences at work.

Places that were frequently occupied by Egypt, and coastal cities that traded regularly with Egypt, often had more evident elements of Egyptian culture. Egypt was always on the alert, through a spy network, to any sign of an impending invasion of Egypt proper, or to the rise of any strong group in Canaan. It would send armies across Canaan to meet those threats. Egypt also invaded Canaan periodically as an easy source of loot and slaves; and it stationed troops in outposts near the borders with Canaan, and even inside those borders.

As we noted before, the plagues, the Passover, and the Exodus occurred during the long rule in Egypt of the great Pharaoh Rameses II. The Pharoah that followed Rameses II, Merneptah, often invaded Canaan just to loot. Several of his battles were recorded on an engraved stone, or stele. In 1207 BC, in the fifth year of his reign, Merneptah led an army into western Canaan and pillaged two cities there. Then, out in the open countryside, he came across a small band of armed men, and his army killed them.

Merneptah recorded on his stele that these men were Israelites. In fact, this stele has the first-ever recorded use of the word *Israel* as a name for a community. The discovery of the stele was made in 1896 by one of the best of the early archae-ologists, Flinders Petrie. He said of his discovery: *"And won't the reverends be pleased!"* They were, and the rabbis were ecstatic!

One of Canaan's most interesting areas, and one of the most troublesome to the Jews, was the coastal plain. It was controlled by the cities of two different groups of people who had mastered the art of building and sailing ships. One of these seafaring groups were old-time Canaanites, having lived there on the coast for more than 1,000 years before the Exodus, so as early as 2,300 BC. We know them by the name they made famous all over the Mediterranean, the Phoenicians, and they spoke a Semitic language that had some similarity to Hebrew.

The Greek name for their part of Canaan's coast—the northern part—was Phoenicia, and my teachers had always suggested that the name meant *"the land of the purple,"* from the Phoenicians' manufacture and trade in purple dye, and in cloth that had been dyed purple. However, linguists now say that Phoenicia actually meant *"land of the red-haired people,"* and that creates all kinds of conjectures as to their origin. Physical anthropologists now say that if you have red hair, your ancestors almost certainly originated in northern or northwestern Europe. When Egyptian artists portrayed Phoenician foot soldiers on the walls of tombs, they painted them with red hair.

Over time, the Phoenicians conquered all the cities on the northern coastal plain, and built some new ones. On the coast, their main cities were Tyre, Sidon, Byblos, and Beirut, but they had other cities in Canaan, as well. These sea-faring people also built cities all around the edge of the Mediterranean, including such memorable ones as Carthage, Barcelona, Marseilles, and Genoa.

The Phoenicians made fortunes through trade, much of it in wine, and much of that trade was with Egypt. Accordingly, their cities would have small Egyptian temples to accommodate visiting Egyptian traders or any emissaries of the pharaoh.

The Phoenicians had conquered and made their own the old city of Byblos, part of an empire centered on Ebla. Byblos' main trading items were papyrus scrolls ready for writing. The early books of the Bible were written on them. The Greeks named these scrolls *bublos,* after the city of Byblos, and from that word we got the word *"Bible"* and the word *"book."*

As noted earlier, the Phoenicians dominated the northern coastal plain. The Israelites, moving from east to west, would eventually control the central part of the coast as well, but the coastline had very few harbors from which a seafaring city might develop. Originally, it was inhabited by other Canaanites.

On the southern coastal plain there was a group of aggressive newcomers, the Philistines. The Egyptians feared these invaders, but managed to fight them off around 1190 BCE. Shortly after that, the pharoah permitted the Philistines to remain on the south coast of Canaan. In return, they made annual payments of tribute to the pharoah, and sent him a full set of Philistine bodyguards. They were trusted because they were less likely to be a part of any priestly plot to assassinate the ruler. Also, the bodyguards knew they would forfeit their own lives if that should happen.

The Philistines were bad news for the Hebrew/Israelite newcomers, and vice versa. They were both trying to take over the same territory at the same time. The Philistines were moving inland from the southwestern coast, and the Israelites were moving inland from the southeastern hill country. Both wanted control of the fairly well-watered central hill country between them. It could produce grain, sheep and goats, oil from olives, and wine from vineyards on the slopes of hills facing the sun, and slaves—an important commodity for both groups.

It was inevitable that the Philistines and Israelites would collide and fight, and hate each other with a passion. Our ideas about the Philistines come almost entirely from the stories the Jews told about them, so we wound up with the notion that the very name *"Philistine"* suggested a barbarian. But the Philistines had similar feelings about the Israelites, for some very good reasons. For one thing, the Philistine artisans, in particular the pottery makers and the metal workers, were much more advanced than those of their contemporary Israelite artisans.

Also, in contrast to the Israelites, the Philistines *elected* their leaders and had the good sense to form a tight confederation of city states that extended from about where Tel Aviv is today down to the Gaza Strip. The Israelites fell back on that old Sumerian custom of calling up a king to organize their tribes for a fight against the army of the Philistine confederation.

Like the Phoenicians, the Philistines were good sailors, and the Egyptians acknowledged that by calling them *The Sea People*. In southeastern Turkey, the Philistines had learned from the Hittites how to make and use iron weapons. The Israelites didn't even have iron, so they lost a lot of battles to the Philistines, who dominated them for about 200 years.

Beyond their iron battle axes and spears, the Philistines had something else the Israelites desperately needed—iron digging tools, and iron knives and plowshares. The Philistines let them have this iron hardware, but under a strict rule that must have been deeply humiliating. The Israelites were required to use Philistine blacksmiths to repair any broken iron tools, and they could go only once a year to a Philistine city to get everything sharpened.

According to a story in the Bible, one of the first things David did when he became king was to set up his own iron smelter. Well, the Israelites did prevail over the Philistines, ultimately, but the Philistines kept a homeland state until about 700 BCE. They were finally absorbed by the larger population of Jews and other Canaanites, after some 500 years in what we know as Palestine.

Modern Israel is in the heart of old Canaan and, in recent times, the most commonly unearthed images of a deity have been those of the goddess Ishtar—the old Babylonian transformation of the Sumerian goddess Inanna. In very early days in Canaan, she had the name Ishtar, but then was renamed over time by one or another of the 14 groups who spoke different languages in Canaan at the time.

In Hebrew, Ishtar was either Asherah or Ashtoreth; in Greek, she became Astarte, and then Aphrodite; but she was still Inanna in the way that she was worshipped. All of these goddesses were identified with the Evening Star, which we and the Romans call Venus. And each of them carried Inanna's original title, *Queen of Heaven.* This goddess, whatever the name given her, remained popular throughout Canaan and in nearby areas of Sumerian culture.

It is worth mentioning again: One of the reasons why this goddess remained so popular was that she was the first deity in ancient mythology to make a covenant with the earth's people. After Enki, the Sumerian god of water, nearly destroyed everyone with the great flood, Inanna promised the survivors that such a thing would never happen again, if they would agree to be a just and righteous people.

Remember how the Prophet Ezekiel complained bitterly because the women of Jerusalem were still weeping for Tammuz? Tammuz was the name Hebrews and others used for Dumuzi, the Sumerian god loved by Inanna. Ezekiel died in 570 BCE in Babylon during the Babylonian Captivity. That was some 2,500 years after the Sumerians began to worship Inanna, the Queen of Heaven, and tell of her separation from Dumuzi. Incidentally, in one of the many ironies of history and religion, and in spite of the obvious connection to the idolatrous myth that so infuriated Ezekiel, Tammuz is still the *official name* of the fourth month of the Jewish calendar year, and rabbis still recognize it as a Babylonian name.

In fact, all the official names of the months of the orthodox Jewish calendar are closely derived from the corresponding names of the months of the Babylonian calendar. The Hebrew people absorbed much in their brief Babylonian captivity. Perhaps that is why they all stayed on in Babylon for 18 years after Cyrus freed them. Even then, fewer than half the Jews chose to return to their homeland.

In Mesopotamian culture areas, morality and spirituality were mutually reinforcing, and so they were in Canaan. At the top of the pantheon of deities in Canaan was the Supreme God *EL*, Lord of the Earth. His original Sumerian equivalent, again back some 2,500 years in time, was Enlil, now morphed into El.

El was wise, caring, compassionate, and merciful. El was the Supreme Judge of all things, and he expected justice and righteousness to prevail on earth. El didn't mind being represented in stone.

Figure 37: The Canaanite god, El, seated on his throne

Genesis 33:20 says that El was the God of Israel, but that took some time to happen. It is clear from ancient names, however, that El made a major impact on the Hebrew people: Bethel means *"Home of El,"* Daniel—*"El is the Judge,"* Ezekiel—*"El strengthens,"* Ishmael—*"El has heard,"* and

Samuel means *"Asked of El."* In all, there are 113 biblical names with El in them.

The very name Israel means *"to struggle with El,"* and was given to Jacob after his all-night wrestle with God. But he wasn't the first to be called Israel! Clay tablets found across Canaan recorded the name Israel long before the Bible was written, along with most of those other names with El built in. One clay tablet, some 4,000 years old but only found in 2011, noted that Israel was the name of an Akkadian boy, so it was not reserved for Hebrews. To date, that is the oldest known use of the name.

Over time, El simply became the Israelite name for God. The prophet Elijah's name means *"El is Yah,"* and that represents an important step forward in the religious history of the Jews. When Moses fled Egypt after killing the cruel slave-master, he hid out among the Midianites in south-eastern Canaan, who led him to their storm god, Yah. If he wanted, Yah could alleviate drought.

In Canaan, that was a bit of a problem for the Hebrews, because the Great God El had a son who was a storm god, and his name was *BA'AL*. Ba'al's name comes into Canaan from the Babylonian storm god Marduk, whose name became so holy that it was never pronounced. Instead, Marduk was referred to only as BEL, which simply meant "LORD," in the Akkadian language. In Canaan, Bel morphed into Ba'al.

Canaanite mythology, following earlier Mesopotamian myths, said that the god Ba'al had created lightning and thunder so the gods and goddesses would know when it was going to rain. As a storm god competing with Yah, Ba'al had to go, for that and other good reasons. For example, Ba'al's temples provided courtesans for more men than those of any other god providing such a service. Incidentally, that Canaanite goddess Asherah was the wife of El, and for these heavily partriarchal Hebrews, she had to go too.

But something else had happened. The Hebrews' view of God was maturing, due in part to their long stay in Egypt. Nature gods were no longer needed; they were no longer relevant to their elevated understanding of God. All those positive attributes of El—wise, caring, compassionate, and interested in justice and mercy for all—reinforced their recent exposure to Akhenaten's notion that there was only one god. As *Deuteronomy* put it in about 622 BC, *"There is none like unto God!"* So Yah went from being a subordinate god, to one so great that he becomes El. El is who Yah is. EL is YAH! Elijah!

CHAPTER EIGHTEEN
Captivity

Captivity in Babylon wasn't the first disaster to afflict the people of the little states of Judah and Israel. In 721 BCE, the Assyrians sacked Israel and carried off 27,290 leading citizens, who they sold into slavery to countries to the East. These were the *Ten Lost Tribes of Israel.*

After that disaster, there was only one kingdom left, Judah, and it suffered a similar fate, beginning with a raid by Nebuchadnezzar I in 605 BCE. He also carried off large numbers of Jews to be sold as slaves. Then Jerusalem was captured eight years later, in 597 BCE, by Nebuchadnezzar, with perhaps 10,000 more taken into captivity.

The worst comes from Nebuchadnezzar II, who destroyed Jerusalem in 586 BCE and carried off 18,000 more of its people. The rest fled to the countryside. The affluent and important folks were in captivity in Babylon, where a "new" old religion was on the rise. It was Zoroastrianism, brought in by traders, captives, and even by missionaries from Persia. Indeed, the Hebrews will be rescued and permitted to return to Judah, by an ardent Zoroastrian—the new conqueror of Babylon, Cyrus the Great of Persia. Cyrus not only released the Hebrews from captivity in Babylon, he gave them a new identity: "*Jews*", because so many of them came from Judah.

If for no other reason, people would be interested in the religious beliefs of someone rescuing them from slavery. These beliefs would affect the future of their own religion and that of Christianity, which was yet to come. Among the main ideas of that faith are the free-will choice between good and evil, monotheism, and false gods. If the linguists are correct in dating the origins of Zoroastrianism to about 1500 BCE, Zarathustra was preaching monotheism in Persia even before Akhenaten in Egypt. However, the Sumerians had at least a 1,000-year head-start over the Zoroastrians in believing that man was given a free-will choice between good and evil.

After only three generations in Babylon, and eighteen years after being freed, a small portion of the captive Jews chose to return to Judah. Their leader was a Jew with a distinctly Babylonian name: *Zerubabbel*. Zerubabbel means, in Akkadian, "*the seed of Babylon.*" Those elders who wanted to return had good reason to be worried.

Once the temple was rebuilt in Jerusalem, the Jews began to accelerate the recording of their spiritual history as they remembered it. That had started earlier with an assembled copy of *Deuteronomy*, probably working with earlier versions that have not been found or reported. The first known copy of *Deuteronomy* was dropped in the temple offering box in Jerusalem in 621 BCE. Then, after the Captivity, the other books began to emerge back in Judah.

We should know that as the time of Jesus came closer, there was a deep division between Judaism's two major groups: the Pharisees and the Sadducees. The Pharisees were lay scholars, teachers and leaders who based their authority on control of the synagogues. The Sadducees were aristocrats—priests and lay noblemen—who based their authority on their long-standing control of the temple in Jerusalem. These two groups, the Pharisees and the Sadducees, were the two main groups in the Sanhedrin, the ruling council of Judea established by the Roman conquerors.

The Pharisees had absorbed and were promoting major Zoroastrian notions: belief in angels and demons, judgment after death, punishment after death for your accumulated sins, resurrection, and a coming messiah with a millennium of peace and justice to follow. The name *Pharisee* may well have come from the language of the Persians, *Farsi*.

In sharp contrast to the Pharisees, the Sadducees said, in effect: There is no immortality of the soul, no resurrection, no afterlife, no judgment, no punishment after death, no Messiah coming soon, no angels, and no demons! Well, guess who won? The Pharisees! The Romans destroyed Jerusalem and the temple in 70 CE, something the Sadducees had said could never happen. And that marked the end of the Sadducees as a religious force in Israel.

By 120 CE, 50 years later, the Pharisees had chosen and assembled the books of the Hebrew bible. Christians later would accept this as their Old Testament, with basically the same content, but reorganized in terms of which books went where. The Old Testament had been a long time in the making, and its compelling ideas, lasting values and eternal truths had been distilled from many sources.

2011 CE was the 400th anniversary of that extraordinary translation, the *King James Bible*. It is still alive with an intense spirituality, and is elegantly beautiful as literature. Scholars still work to make the Bible as accurate as possible. More recently, gender equality in the language used has become an important concern. Someday soon, there should be a new *New Revised Standard Edition*.

CHAPTER NINETEEN
An Afterword or Two

In 1934, the archaeologist James Starkey was excavating a site in the ruins of Lachise, an old fortified city west of Hebron, in Judea. In the rubbish heap of an old temple, he uncovered the shattered remains of an ancient piece of Canaanite pottery. It is called *The Lachise Ewer.* This vase depicted, among other things, a ram—symbol of the Great God *EL.*

Figure 38: The Lachise Ewer

Also on the vase were a pair of seven-branched trees. That symbol—the sacred seven-branched tree—would eventually be adopted by the Israelites as a symbol for *YAH*. It would also be introduced as the menorah, in later times. But long before all that, it had another meaning. The earliest sacred trees were representations of the cosmology of the Sumerians, their *Tree of Life*.

The Akkadians, the Babylonians, and all who came after them in Mesopotamia made similar images. The sun god was the central trunk branch, the moon god and Venus were the first two lower branches on either side of the trunk, and then Mars, Mercury, Jupiter, and Saturn, and their respective deities, were distributed as the other four branches above Venus and the moon.

Some versions of the tree had four branches on each side of the trunk-branch; some had four on one side and three on the other. The number of gods and goddesses represented as branches varied with the artist, but the sun god was the stem, and the moon god and Venus were the branches near the base. Inanna, Goddess of Heaven, was represented by the branch assigned to Venus in the initial mythology.[68]

**Figure 39: Early Cylinder Seal, with
Inanna and the Sacred Tree**

In Canaan, one of the sequential representations of Inanna as Goddess of Heaven was Asherah, female counterpart of the great god *EL*. El was the *creator,* and Asherah was the *creatrix*. Asherah was known for her love of trees. Sacred trees were often used to represent her, and they appear together with her written name.

Figure 40: Asherah figurines from the ninth to seventh centuries BCE found in various parts of Jerusalem

When Loraine and I moved back to Austin after 13 years in the Boston area, we rejoined University Christian Church, located just across from the University of Texas campus. In our absence, the church had established a Foundation for Creative Ministry. Knowing that we had recently retired, a friend who helped establish the foundation asked if we would develop an exhibition of Judeo-Christian visual art—painting and sculpture—to be held in the church.

He knew that we had once selected some 500 modern paintings and sculpture from India for a Dallas-based gallery. (Some of those had content derived from Christian beliefs, or came from the artists' understanding that Gandhi once considered becoming a Christian.) Loraine agreed to hang the paintings and display the sculpture, but it was up to me to find these visions of faith.

As I had no idea who these artists might be, I simply called the leading museums and galleries in large cities in the U.S. and asked the head curators whether they knew of good contemporary artists in their region whose primary interest was the expression of religious ideas and themes. There was only one "Hell, no!" answer—most gave positive responses. If there *was* enthusiasm expressed for an artist, I identified the next most prominent museum or gallery in that area, and asked the same question. When two top curators mentioned the same person, I contacted the artist, and asked for slides. My method was inexact, but reasonably effective.

After Loraine and I viewed the artwork on our home screen, we chose the artists to be in the exhibition. I asked the artist whether the pieces we had selected from the slides, or very similar recent work, could be available for an exhibition in the Fall of 1986. At the end of our search, we had an exhibition of 92 paintings and sculpture by 13 artists, with an exhibition title of *The Eighth Day of Creation*. That appropriate name was taken from a quotation by Nicholas Berdyaev, a Russian Orthodox theologian and philosopher.

One of the sculptures was a magnificent wall-sized menorah done by Gregor Goethals, a professor at the Rhode Island School of Design. She had made the menorah for a large synagogue in Monroe, Louisiana. Professor Goethals kept the original model of the menorah and sent that piece for our exhibition. In a note, she said in effect: *You can light this menorah if you wish, but be certain to use kosher olive oil made for use in menorahs. You <u>must</u> light the lamp of the central stem first. Then light the lamps of the other six stems.*

Well, we weren't about to risk a fire in the midst of all these borrowed works of art, but we were certainly pleased to have such a beautifully sculptured menorah in the two-week exhibition. The *"Eighth Day"* attracted 1,100 visitors.

There are numerous scholarly articles suggesting that the arms of the menorah represent the days of the week. And we remember that, after the Sun's day, the days of the week were named for the moon god, then the Goddess Inanna as Venus, and then the gods of the four other planets first identified by the Sumerians.

About three years ago, I was teaching my SAGE seminar, *"Ancient Civilization as Biblical Background."* On a sudden hunch, after remembering the exhibition, I searched some knowledgeable Hebrew sources to see if that all-important central stem of a Jewish menorah had a name. It does. Its name is *SHAMASH*, the Akkadian/Babylonian Sun God.

Figure 41. Drawn from an early cylinder seal bas-relief of Shamash (circa 2015 BCE)

APPENDICES

A. *FROM HABIRU TO HEBREW?*

Much has been written by biblical scholars on the origin of the word "Hebrew." In particular, did the word stem from the Sumerian/Akkadian word "Habiru?" One of the most detailed of such efforts was by Nadav Na'aman in his article *"Habiru and Hebrew: The Transfer of a Social Term to the Literary Sphere,"* which appeared in the Journal of Near Eastern Studies, Vol. 45, No. 4, (Oct.1986, 271-288.) His circuitous argument seems to conclude that "Hebrew" was not directly derived from "Habiru." However, there are other viewpoints on the issue.

My reading of the literature suggests that, most likely, Hebrew *was* derived from Habiru (Hapiru, also.) In Sumerian and Akkadian, habiru suggested an activity, which was critical to the trade and the food supply of Mesopotamian cities:

to "cross over" arid and semi-arid lands to trade locally-produced goods.

Habiru groups traded for animals herded by nomads on two great plateaus, one to the west in Arabia, and one to the east in what is now Iran. Over time, any group doing this long-distance trading for any length of time would have been identified with that name.

A story concerning a very difficult king of the city of Mari gives a sharp introduction to the Habiru. Mari was an economic and cultural outpost of the city of Ur, but well to the north along the western bank of the Euphrates River in what is now Syria. In 1933, a French archaeological team uncovered a library of some 25,000 clay tablets, including letters to the King and notes by him. Most of these letters were composed between 1800BCE and 1700BCE.

One letter was from a lower-level administrator who was trying to keep peace with a Habiru group in his assigned area that was the target of the king's anger. The group's elders did not want their sons serving in this belligerent ruler's army, so for many years they had paid a special tax to exempt their sons from military service. This harsh king got upset just thinking about that, so he ordered the regional administrator to bring the group's sons into the army.

The worried civil servant wrote a letter to the king, saying: *"If you do that, they will no longer habiru (cross over)!"*—implying that Mari would lose some of its trade and most of the city's meat supply. A sobering document found in the Mari library presented a dated note by the fanatical king saying: *"This is the year I beheaded the leader of the Habiru."*

The Egyptians had allowed many groups to come into the Nile delta area to produce meat for their cities. They gave a single name for all of them—*Apiru*. (The Egyptians had a different name for pastoral nomads—*Shasu*.) On his first sojourn into Egypt, Abraham grew wealthy as an Apiru in the delta, while his wife shared the Pharaoh's bed.

"Abram the Hebrew" is a phrase in *Genesis* 14:13 in early bibles. The 54 scholars who prepared the King James Version of the Bible retained the Geneva Bible's citation of it. That phrase was used in almost all versions of *Genesis*. However, a much earlier text version was prepared in everyday, commonly-used Greek in the city of Alexandria, Egypt.

According to a widely-challenged story, Ptolemy II (Philadelphus), ordered 72 Hebrew scholars to write out the Torah, the first five books of their scriptures, around 250 BCE. As the story goes, the 72 produced 72 identical versions in exactly 72 days. That was more than enough '70s' to give rise to the term *Septuagint*. Regardless of its origin, the English translation of the common Greek used in the early Septuagint for *Genesis* 14:13 was originally cited as *"Abram, who crossed over."* Abram the Habiru became Abram the Hebrew.

Many online sites suggest that the Hebrew word for a "Hebrew" person is ☐☐☐☐ (*eevriy*) and comes from the root word ☐☐☐ (*ever* or *avar*) which is translated *"to cross over."*

B. *ABOUT THOSE SAMARITANS*

Samaria was that central region that reached into both Judah and Israel. Perhaps you have wondered why the Samaritans had such a bad reputation, generally, when there was at least one good Samaritan in the New Testament. Over time, there were several reasons why they were detested by the more orthodox Jews.

The first is that, after conquering the area in 721 BCE, the Assyrians chose Samaria as a site for resettling some of their conquered people from areas far from Canaan. This was a tactical move to lower the probability of organized rebellion in both areas. Also, in this poor terrain, the transplanted people were not likely to become prosperous, and were therefore less dangerous. So Samaria had a reduced Jewish population and a significant number of people foreign to that region. Intermarriage was more than a possibility.

The second reason for Jewish scorn of the Samaritans came just after the return in 583 BCE of some of the Jews in captivity in Babylon. The governor of Samaria actually protested the rebuilding of Jerusalem. Officials in Samaria were in control of all of Judah and wanted to keep it that way. Naturally, this was deeply resented by the former captives because, to their way of thinking, if you don't rebuild Jerusalem, the Holy City of God, there would be no temple.

A third reason developed about 400 BCE, when the Jewish priestly class in Samaria spurned an order from the high priesthood in Jerusalem. The directive ordered all Samaritan priests to follow the example of the priesthood in Jerusalem and get rid of all non-Jewish wives. Many Samaritan priests had married women from the displaced group brought in by the Assyrians and other non-Jews, so collectively they ignored all orders from Jerusalem from that time on.

Even worse was an act of defiance that occurred after Alexander the Great conquered Canaan on his way to Egypt. In the ultimate rebellious act, Samaritans built their own temple on Mount Gerizim. Only Jerusalem was supposed to have a temple. The Samaritans had gone too far.

All these would have been more than enough to ostracize the Samaritans, but there was one final act of rebellion. As the canon for the Hebrew Bible, the *Tanakh,* developed, the Samaritans announced that they would never consider anything as scripture except the *Torah*, those first five books.

Interestingly enough, there is still a small community of Samaritans around the town of Nablus in Israel.

C. ZOROASTRIAN BELIEFS

The ideas, practices, and beliefs of this early Persian religion included the following:

1. Monotheism
2. The concept of "false gods"
3. The coming of a savior
4. A coming millennium of great peace
5. The practice of baptism (but long after its development in Egypt)
6. The notion of a soul and its transmigration (also after Egypt)
7. Communion as a sacrament
8. Angels, including seven archangels
9. The concept of a devil or demonic force leading the fight against heaven
10. The notion of a heavenly book in which human deeds are recorded
11. A day of last judgment, with a resurrection of the body (actually, a *re-creation* of it)

Note: Zoroastrianism may also have been an ideological forerunner of certain tenets of Buddhism, given Zoroaster's dictum of *"Good thoughts, good words, good deeds."*

D. *OUR COSMIC LEGACY*

The Sumerians knew, and worshipped as gods and goddesses, the sun and the moon and the five planets they had identified from their movement in the night sky: Mars, Mercury, Jupiter, Venus, and Saturn. Each was associated with a Sumerian deity, and of course they had Sumerian names, not the planetary names familiar to us.

These seven underpinned the fundamental belief system for all of Mesopotamia, with only name changes over time. This structure would spread to many of Mesopotamia's nearby areas, including Canaan. We still have their legacy: look at our days of the week, and the deities we unconsciously honor every seven days. They boil down to a similar set of seven worshipped by the Sumerians, with the deities chosen locally, but the seven heavenly bodies remained the same. This pattern was arranged by the Sumerians around 3000 BCE.

OUR DAYS OF THE WEEK WITH ASSOCIATED CELESTIAL BODIES AND DEITIES

SUNDAY (Sun)	God of the Sun's day
Monday (Moon)	God or Goddess of the Moon's day
Tuesday (Mars)	God of War and Sky (Germanic) Tiu's Day)

WEDNESDAY (Mercury)	<u>God of the Hunt (Anglo-Saxon) Woden's Day</u>
THURSDAY (Jupiter)	<u>God of Thunder (Norse) Thor's Day</u>
FRIDAY (Venus)	<u>Goddess of Love (Germanic) Freya's Day</u>
SATURDAY (Saturn)	<u>God of Agriculture (Roman) Saturn's Day</u>

E. *A WORKING CHRONOLOGY: FROM UR TO THE BABYLONIAN CAPTIVITY*

<u>After 2380 BCE</u>:

A part of Abraham's ancestral group settle in Ur shortly after the conquest of Sumeria by Sargon I, the leader of a different Semitic tribe centered on the city of Akkad whose ruins have yet to be discovered.

By 2004 BCE:

Abraham's father, Terah, leaves Ur with his family to avoid a forthcoming conquest by the Elamites. After a long journey, he and his family settle in Haran, in what is now southeastern Turkey (their ancestral homeland before Israel). Terah dies, and Abraham (Abram) becomes the group's patriarch.

By 1825 BCE:

An Abraham, who is a direct descendant of the patriarch and named for him as was the custom of the day, leads his extended family to Canaan.

By 1820 BCE:

Due to persistent drought, Abraham fails to establish a permanent settlement in Canaan. All move to Egypt, where Sarah enters the harem of the Pharaoh. Abraham prospers in the well-watered delta of the Nile, which is open to outsiders who produce cattle for Egyptian cities.

By 1800 BCE:

The Pharaoh discovers Abraham's deception regarding Sarah and banishes him and all his family. They return to Canaan.

<u>By 1750 BCE</u>:

A west-Asian people, the Hyksos, along with other pastoralist allies, move into Lower Egypt, which includes the very large delta of the Nile. They have already crossed Canaan, and have recruited many non-Hyksos for their armies. Those armies are impressive and successful, as they have the first horse-drawn war chariots ever to enter the region.

The Hyksos conquer all of Egypt, but establish a puppet government in Upper Egypt in the south. The Hyksos capital and power base remains in Lower Egypt in the north. (Egypt's counter-intuitive political geography makes sense only when one remembers that the upper and lower terms were basic references to the all-important Nile.)

<u>By 1715 BCE</u>:

Jacob's son, Joseph, is sold by his brothers and taken to Lower Egypt. He prospers there under Hyksos rule. However, on behalf of the non-Egyptian Pharaoh ruling over Lower Egypt, Joseph drives the Egyptian peasantry into landless poverty and slavery. Only Egyptian priests are able to keep their land and animals. (*Genesis*, Chapter 47.)

By 1700 BCE:

Jacob's other sons come to Lower Egypt in search of food, and the whole family moves to Egypt. They settle in Goshen in the eastern delta of the Nile in Lower Egypt. (As noted before, the Bible states that the Hebrew people remained in Egypt 430 years. This chronology follows that assertion.)

1575 BCE:

The Egyptians in Upper Egypt (southern Egypt) rebel and drive out the Hyksos. The Hebrews are identified as Hyksos collaborators and are enslaved.

1279 BCE:

Rameses II becomes Pharaoh. Hebrew slaves work on two "warehouse" cities, Rameses and Pithom, both in Goshen in the Nile delta area of Lower Egypt. These were supply depots commonly built for the use of the government, including the military.

By 1270 BCE:

Moses leads the Hebrew people out of Egypt and into the wilderness, but is forced to move on into the hill country east of the Jordan River. With low rainfall, the area is comparatively unproductive.

<u>By 1230 BCE</u>:

Egyptian records mention the destruction of the cities of Canaan, as the Hebrew settlers push into the more productive, wetter areas west of the Jordan.

<u>1207 BCE</u>: Egyptian records make the first-ever use of the word "Israel" in regard to an open-country battle.

<u>1000-925 BCE</u>:

Israel's *Golden Age* of David and Solomon. David declares Jerusalem to be *The City of God*.

<u>721 BCE</u>:

Some 90,000 Israelites (27,000 men and their families) are taken as captives to northern Mesopotamia by the Assyrians. Many are resettled in other conquered lands by their captors.

<u>597 BCE, 586 BCE</u>:

Many more captives are taken, this time to Babylon, from the two kingdoms: Israel in the north and Judah in the south. Jerusalem is destroyed by Nebuchadnezzar, a *neo-Babylonian* ruler.

538 BCE:

Cyrus the Great, the Persian who conquered Babylon, releases the captives and refers to them as "Jews," due to their association with Judah. After 18 more years, most of the Jews opt to stay in Babylon, but some do return and rebuild Jerusalem. After three generations in Babylon, a high priority for them is the completion of their spiritual history.

Note: The worldwide diaspora (dispersal) of the Jews is most often associated with the neo-Babylonian conquests of 597 BCE and 586 BCE. However, the *Ten Lost Tribes of Israel* were scattered in the earlier Assyrian conquest of 721 BCE. It would seem appropriate to date the Jewish diaspora as beginning with that event.

F. *LOSSES BEYOND THE LIVES*

Americans should keep in mind a tragedy that we could easily have prevented. Most of us have read or heard of the destructive looting of Iraq's National Museum in Baghdad. (Our Secretary of Defense at the time, Donald Rumsfeld, shrugged off this ravaging of some of the world's most significant cultural treasures with the convenient throw-away line: *"Stuff happens."*) Fortunately, some of the Museum's priceless antiquities were quickly recovered by U.S. and Iraqi forces, but many were not. The ever-growing losses of this evidence to human history are devastating.

In the last years of the war, large bands of well-organized and well-armed hoodlums looted mounds all over Iraq, including those previously untouched. Looters are still operating in force under the protection of AK-47's, and few of the looted antiquities have been recovered. Officials in Iraq's Bureau of Educational and Cultural Affairs suggested that at least 600,000 items have been stolen, and that was several years ago. The terrorist group ISIS is active in such plunder.

One of the biggest losses relates to the pilfering of a previously unknown Sumerian city's cemetery found just before the war began. As yet unidentified, the city had a cemetery with some 200,000 graves. Looting them has easily provided artifacts for a ready but illicit market in Europe, Asia, and North America. Most of these stolen items leave Iraq through Iran, Jordan, or Syria. The looters look for jewelry and intact pottery, but any interesting object has a buyer.

One U. S. Marine said he purchased eight Sumerian cylinder seals from a street vendor in Baghdad for a few dollars. On his return to the U.S., and after learning more of the sad looting of artifacts in Iraq, he gave the seals to the FBI to be returned to Iraq. He was told later that the cash value of the seals was approximately $30,000, according to prices being paid in Europe. Toward the end of the war, an American colonel concerned over the looting estimated that as many as 15,000 sellable objects were being taken from the ground each day.

NOTES

CHAPTER 1

[1]One evening, we were sitting with friends in the front row of a large hall at the Dell Jewish Community Center in Austin, Texas. We were part of a full house listening to a visiting rabbi comment on what he believed to be new discoveries about *Genesis*. The gentleman who introduced him suggested that the speaker would talk for 50 minutes or so. Instead, he droned on for almost two hours, presenting nothing we could discern as new information. A prepared meal on tables in the back waited for him to finish.

He was asked twice by the moderator to close, but instead of wrapping up, the rabbi plunged ahead with a long-winded rationalization for Abraham's less than manly actions as he entered Egypt for the first time. When the rabbi said: *"Now Abraham, as a husband...,"* he was cut off in mid-sentence by a woman seated directly behind us who screamed at the top of her lungs: *"SUCKS!"* That soon brought an end to a long, weak lecture, and the meal that followed was fine.

[2] Pierre Teilhard de Chardin, *The Future of Man* (New York: Image, 1964), 307.

[3] Peter Ward and Donald Brownlee, *Rare Earth: Why Complex Life is Uncommon in the Universe* (New York: Springer, 2000).

[4] Kate Melville, *"Twenty-five Years, and ET hasn't called back,"* science-agogo.com, 22nd Nov., 1999.

[5] In discussing the Universe in relation to religion as developed on our little planet, the awesome physicist Richard Feynman once remarked that the stage was too large for the drama.

[6] Will Durant, *The Story of Civilization. Vol. 1: Our Oriental Heritage*; Simon and Schuster, New York, 1954, p 116.

CHAPTER 2

[7] In 2006, Israeli archaeologists found eight teeth dating to the same time period in a cave east of Tel Aviv. Most likely, they belonged to that same defunct line of early Homo sapiens spear-makers. They were not us.

[8] *National Geographic News*, October 28, 2010.

CHAPTER 3

[9] For a very readable account of early language development and diffusion based on DNA evidence, read Steven Olson's *Mapping Human History*. (Steve Olson, *Mapping Human History*, Mariner Books, New York, 2003.) One of the more interesting themes in his book is that, in terms of DNA differentials, the idea of "race" is absolutely meaning-

less. All *Homo sapiens sapiens* are very much alike, genetically—there are no significant differences.

[10] Incidentally, that "third of all modern medicine" phrase is a good example of the many kinds of selective decisions one has to make. One very reputable source said 40% of all modern pharmaceuticals are plant-based, and another equally respected source said 25%. It seemed reasonable to split things down the middle and say "perhaps a third."

[11] Jared Diamond's *Guns, Germs, and Steel,* gives a detailed account of animal domestication and its meaning for human development.

[12] Unhappily, we have been writing down our thoughts about religion for only 5,300 years. See Merlin Stone's interesting book, *When God Was a Woman*. There are a number of other texts with somewhat similar themes.

[13] Here I should mention that early nomadic groups kept mostly sheep and goats, but never pigs. The keeping of pigs was a prime cultural separator between the shepherd and the farmer. That may have contributed to early dietary restrictions by nomadic groups.

CHAPTER 4

[14] James Mellaart, "A Neolithic City in Turkey." *Scientific American*, April, 1964, p. 9. See also his book, *Catal Huyuk: A Neolithic Town in Anatolia* (McGraw-Hill Book Co., New York, 1967) for astounding displays of wall painting, among many other interesting features.

[15] Mellaart, "A Neolithic City in Turkey," p. 79. In Sumerian tombs, women were often buried with their obsidian beads.

[16] Will Durant, *Our Oriental Heritage*, Vol. 1 of 11, *The Story of Civilization*, Simon and Schuster, New York, 1935. I am indebted, also, to my University of Texas colleague Gideon Sjoberg for insights drawn from his classic text, *The Preindustrial City: Past and Present* (Free Press, New York, 1960).

CHAPTER 5

[17] Having had the opportunity to observe farming in several parts of the developing world—India, China, Brazil, Senegal, and Egypt from 1957 to 1984, I can attest that none of the poor farmers planting grain had seed drills. Some were still throwing their seed broadcast, which is the least efficient of all the ways to plant grain.

[18] Roberts, Thorton, and Pigott, "Development of Metallurgy in Eurasia," *Antiquity* 83 (2009), pp. 1012-1022.

[19] Much later, the Greeks would call these five planets "the wandering stars." Sumerian astronomers also described something "very bright" that "passed over" periodically. They called it *Nibra*, but it sounds like Halley's Comet to us.

[20] "Wedge-shaped," from the Latin *cuneus*, meaning "wedge."

[21] See William N. Goetzmann, *The Origins of Value: The Financial Innovations That Created Modern Capital Markets* (with K.G. Rouwenhorst, ed.) Oxford University Press, New York, 2005.

CHAPTER 6

[22] Will Durant, *Our Oriental Heritage*, Vol. 1 of 11, *The Story of Civilization*, Simon and Schuster, New York, 1935, p. 161.

[23] Wolfgang Helck, *Amenemhet I, King of Egypt*, Harrassowitz, Wiesbaden, 1969, p. 236.

[24]*The Book of Esther*, which was the only Old Testament book not included in the Dead Sea Scrolls—possibly because it was written by a woman, concerns Esther's saving the Jews from deadly prejudice in Susa and its Elamite empire. Whether *Esther* is history or a novella is of little consequence—it is a great story, good enough to get a holiday declared in its honor: *Purim*.

CHAPTER 7

[25] Jeremy Black and Anthony Green, *Gods, Demons and Symbols of Ancient Mesopotamia*, University of Texas Press, Austin, 1992, p. 109.

[26]J. Black and A. Green, *Gods, Demons and Symbols*, p. 76.

[27] Samuel Noah Kramer, *History Begins at Sumer*, Univ. of Pennsylvania Press, Philadelphia, 1981, pp. 80-81.

[28] In the flexible, changeable mythology of Sumeria, Inanna's father has ranged from Enlil to Enki to Nanna, and even to *AN*, the original father of deities in Sumeria. (In the Akkadian language, An became *Anu*.)

[29] Gurney, O.R., and Kramer, S.N., *Sumerian Literary Texts in the Ashmolean Museum,* Oxford University Press: Oxford, 1976, pp 74-76.

[30] Adapted from *Hymn to Nanshe*, lines 20-31, from Black, J.A., Cunningham, G., Fluckiger-Hawker, E., Robson, E., and Zólyomi, G., *The Electronic Text Corpus of Sumerian Literature* (http://www-etcsl.orient.ox.ac.uk/), Oxford 1998.

[31] Black, J.A., Cunningham, G., Fluckiger-Hawker, E., Robson, E., and Zólyomi, G., *The Electronic Text Corpus of Sumerian Literature* (http://www-etcsl.orient.ox.ac.uk/), Oxford 1998, lines 224-231.

CHAPTER 8

[32] Samuel Noah Kramer, *History Begins at Sumer*, University of Pennsylvania Press, Philadelphia, 1994, p. 92. (Adapted from Kramer's translation)

[33] From Kramer, *The Sumerians*, p, 116.

[34] James B. Pritchard, ed. *The Ancient Near East, An Anthology of Texts & Pictures*, Princeton University Press, Princeton, 2011. p. 335. (From the translation by Kramer)

[35] Diane Wolkstein and Samuel Noah Kramer, *INANNA, Queen of Heaven and Earth: Her Stories and Hymns from Sumer*, Harper and Row, New York, 1983, p. 103.

[36] Adapted from "Counsels of Wisdom," translated by Robert Biggs, in James B. Pritchard, ed., *The Ancient Near East, An Anthology of Texts and Pictures*, Princeton University Press, Princeton, 2011, pp.362-364.

[37] From a longer prayer translated by Robert F. Harper, for *The Biblical World*, Ed. William R. Harper, New Series, Vol. XXIII, Jan-June, 1904, Univ. of Chicago Press, Chicago, 1904, pp. 437-439.

CHAPTER 9

[38] Urukagina may have come to power as the leader of a rebellion, as some scholars have suggested.

[39] You can see them in museums in Paris, London, Copenhagen, New York, Philadelphia, Boston (actually, in Cambridge, MA) and Detroit. The Louvre could spare a few—it has nine of the 27.

CHAPTER 10

[40] Gilgamesh is somewhat the prototype of the young king David: physically attractive, but self-centered. Not only were the virgins not safe from this lecherous young man, the virtue of the wives was also in danger. In the Babylonian version of the epic, Gilgamesh is two-thirds god and one-third man, and ruled Uruk for 127 years.

[41] That old radical, The Teacher, may have been remembering this part of the epic story when he wrote in *Ecclesiastes*, Chapter 9, verses 7-10: *"Go thy way, eat thy bread with joy, and drink thy wine with a merry heart; for God now accepteth thy works. Let thy garments be always white; and let thy head lack no ointment. Live joyfully with the wife whom thou lovest all the days of the life of thy vanity, which he hath given thee under the sun, all the days of thy vanity: for that is thy portion in this life, and in thy labour which thou takest under the sun."* (From the King James Version of the Bible, Cambridge edition)

[42] The biblical version of the Great Flood spans 40 days and 40 nights of rain, and then 150 days for the ark to drift on the seas—a very long time considering the problem of feeding the animals. It uses the word "seven" seven times.

CHAPTER 11

[43] From Black, J.A., Cunningham, G., Robson, E., and Zólyomi, G., *The Electronic Text Corpus of Sumerian Literature*, Oxford 1998-; and Arkenberg, J.S., *The Internet Ancient History Sourcebook*, Fordham University. See also the two-volume set compiled by Bendt Alster, *Proverbs of Ancient Sumer: The World's Earliest Proverb Collections,* and Edmund Gordon's collection, *Proverbs: Glimpses of Everyday Life in Ancient Mesopotamia.*

[44] Black, J.A., Cunningham, G., Fluckiger-Hawker, E; Robson, E.; and Zólyomi, G., *The Electronic Text Corpus of Sumerian Literature* (http://www-etcsl.orient.ox.ac.uk/), Oxford, 1998-, lines 1-280.

[45] Bendt Alster, *The Instructions of Shuruppak: A Sumerian Proverb Collection*, (Copenhagen: Akademisk Forlag) 1974.

CHAPTER 12

[46] Samuel Noah Kramer, *The Sumerians: Their History, Culture, and Character*, The University of Chicago Press, Chicago, 1963, Chapter 8, pp. 269-299. He ventured that his list was just "the tip of the iceberg."

[47] Selections from Kramer, *op. cit.* p. 112-124. The list of Sumerian contributions to the Bible largely follows Kramer, but also includes scholarly efforts by others such as Thorkild Jacobsen, Leonard Wooley, Jean Bottero, and Georges Roux.

[48] Georges Roux suggested that, if Dilmun *was* a real place for the Sumerians, then most likely it was the island of Bahrain. Georges Roux, *Ancient Iraq*, second edition, Penguin Books, New York, 1980, p.32.

[49] Although some try to identify this sculpture as Ishtar (Inanna) and label it as such, the descriptive features as a whole apply only to Lilith.

[50] As suggested by the Egyptologist John Romer. John Romer, *Testament: The Bible and History*, Henry Holt and Co., New York, 1993, pp. 30-31. Many of Romer's works have been dramatized for public television.

[51] The idea of a virgin birth seems to have originated with the goddess *INANNA*, who was called "The Virgin Mother," on Sumerian clay tablets. The idea of a virgin birth was also incorporated by some 16 *mystery religions* in regions of the eastern Mediterranean, contemporaneous

with Christianity. The idea was also adopted much earlier by the Zoroastrians in Persia.

[52] Note that the temple feeding the poor worshipped a goddess, not a god.

[53] Again, known in areas impacted by Mesopotamian culture as *Ishtar* and probably *Asherah*.

[54] *Deuteronomy* gives an even earlier version. Also, in a much later instance, Nehemiah, born in Babylon in 444 BCE, not only rebuilt the Temple in Jerusalem, he reinstituted the Law of Jubilee, following the *Deuteronomy* prescription for debt relief at the end of the seventh (Sabbath) year.

[55] *University of Chicago Chronicle*, Volume 15, No. 10, Feb. 1, 1996, from an article by William Harms.

CHAPTER 13

[56] P.J. Vatikiotis, *The History of Modern Egypt*, Fourth Edition, Johns Hopkins Press, Baltimore, 1991.

[57] Modern tests show that the deposited silt layers contained ample amounts of all three of today's most commonly used fertilizers: nitrogen, phosphate, and potash.

[58] Barbara Watterson, *The Egyptians*, Blackwell, Cambridge, Ma., 1997, p.16.

[59] Miriam Lichtheim, *Ancient Egyptian Literature: Vol. I, The Old and Middle Kingdoms*, University of California Press, Berkeley, 1975, p. 69.

CHAPTER 14

[60] In the figure of Ra in his solar boat, note the cross-like *Ankh* that rests on his knee. In Egyptian lore, the Ankh represented immortality. Egypt's Coptic Christians adopted it as their symbol for the Cross.

[61] Thutmose I was the first ruler of the XVIII Dynasty, 1504-1492 BCE, and the first of a line of great warrior kings who restored Egyptian power all the way to Mesopotamia. He was the first pharaoh to make the Egyptian army a life-time profession for young men. Before he created his standing army of volunteers, the army relied on conscripts. Thutmose I was a popular king because he brought so much wealth back into Egypt.

[62] The Place of Truth may have two interpretations—either as the western burial grounds across the Nile from Thebes, or as the nearby ancient village Set Maat, where the workmen, artists, and artisans who worked on the tombs lived separately. Over time, Set Maat became known in Arabic as Deir el-Medina.

CHAPTER 15

[63] Adapted from James B. Pritchard, ed. *The Ancient Near East, An Anthology of Texts & Pictures*, (translator, John A. Wilson, *Egyptian Instructions*). Princeton University Press, Princeton, 2011, p. 346-352.

[64] There was only one Mesopotamian structure listed in the Greek seven-wonder list, and that was not the great ziggurat of Babylon—the "Tower of Babel"—but rather the Hanging Gardens of Babylon.

[65] Adapted from Pritchard, James B., ed., *The Ancient Near East - Volume 1: An Anthology of Texts & Pictures*, (*Hymn to the Aton*, translator John A. Wilson), Princeton, New Jersey: Princeton University Press, 2011, pp. 325-328.

CHAPTER 16

[66]Manetho was the only Egyptian historian to give an account of the exodus of Hebrew slaves. Manetho wrote (in Greek) that an Egyptian priest (unnamed) escorted the slaves out of Egypt after they suffered an outbreak of leprosy. It is important to remember that Manetho lived in the *third century BCE*, long after the event. No historian contemporary to the event made *any* mention of the exodus.

On the subject of Egyptian plagues, perhaps an aside is in order: While I was working on an agricultural project in Egypt in 1981, there was a plague of rats in Lower Egypt—swarms of rats in the countryside, from Cairo to Alexandria. Rats are nocturnal animals, meaning, of course, that normally they are out only after dark. In the middle of the day, just before noon, on a measured one mile of highway, we counted more than 300 rats in the edges of the fields we passed. They were devouring the crops. Rats love the taste of fish, so the Egyptian Agricultural Ministry hurriedly brought in tons of small fish from the Mediterranean. The fish were soaked overnight in a deadly poison, and then scattered in the fields. That immediately reduced the number of rats, but it gave rise to a most terrible smell. There is no way of knowing what other consequences occurred, but the crops were partially saved that year.

CHAPTER 17

[67]Israel Finkelstein and Neil Asher Silberman, *The Bible Unearthed: Archaeology's New Vision of Ancient Israel and the Origin of its Sacred Texts*, The Free Press, New York, 2001.

CHAPTER 19

[68]See Diane Wolkstein and Samuel Noah Kramer, *INANNA, Queen of Heaven and Earth: Her Stories and Hymns from Sumer*, Harper and Row, New York, 1983, pp. 3-9.

BIBLIOGRAPHY

The University of Oxford has compiled an extensive *"Bibliography of Sumerian Literature"* available on-line. Oxford's Electronic Text Corpus of Sumerian Literature is especially helpful. The American University of Cairo has published a series of bibliographies related to both Ancient and Modern Egypt, and these are also accessible on-line. The bibliographies include material relating to the area we identify as Canaan. There are also a number of on-line bibliographies under the titles Ancient Near East and Middle Eastern Studies, and several devoted to Sumeria.

The works cited in the text were my primary sources. The following is an introductory bibliography, selected for the general interests of this particular book.

Bendt Alster, *Proverbs of Ancient Sumer: The World's Earliest Proverb Collections*, Baltimore, 1997.

_____, *The Instructions of Shuruppak, A Sumerian Proverb Collection*, Copenhagen, 1974.

Stephen Bertman, *Handbook to Life in Ancient Mesopotamia*, New York, 2005.

Jeremy Black and Anthony Green, Gods, *Demons and Symbols of Ancient Mesopotamia*, Austin, 1992.

Jean Bottero, *Mesopotamia: Writing, Reasoning, and the Gods*, Chicago, 1992.

James H. Breasted, *The Conquest of Civilization*, New York, 1926.

Teilhard de Chardin, *The Future of Man*, New York, 1964.

James Clottes and David Lewis-Williams, *The Shamans of Prehistory: Trance and Magic in the Painted Caves*, New York, 1996.

John Coulter and Merle C. Coulter, *Where Evolution and Religion Meet*, New York, 1924.

Stephanie Dailey, *Myths from Mesopotamia: Creation, the Flood, Gilgamesh, and Others*, Oxford, 2009.

Jared Diamond, *Guns, Germs, and Steel*, New York, 1997.

Will Durant, *The Story of Civilization, Vol. 1, Our Oriental Heritage*, New York, 1954.

Raymond Faulkner and Ogden Goelet, (trans.), *The Egyptian Book of the Dead: The Book of Going Forth by Day*, San Francisco, 1994.

Israel Finkelstein and Neil Asher Silberman, *The Bible Unearthed: Archaeology's New Vision of Ancient Israel and the Origin of its Sacred Texts*, New York, 2001.

Sigmund Freud, *Moses and Monotheism*, New York, 1939.

Anton Gill, *The Rise and Fall of Babylon: Gateway of the Gods*, New York, 2011.

Jean-Jacques Glassner, (ed. B.R. Foster), *Mesopotamian Chronicles*, Atlanta, 2004.

William Goetzmann, *The Origins of Value: The Financial Innovations That Created Modern Capital Markets*, New York, 2005.

Cyrus H. Gordon and Nahum M. Sarna, *Genesis: World of Myths and Patriarchs*, New York, 1996.

O. R. Gurney and Samuel Noah Kramer, *Sumerian Literary Texts in the Ashmolean Museum*, Oxford, 1976.

Wolfgang Helck, *Amenemhet I, King of Egypt*, Wiesbaden, 1969.

Thorkild Jacobsen, *The Harps That Once. . . Sumerian Poetry in Translation*, New Haven, 1987.

_____, *The Treasures of Darkness: A History of Mesopotamian Religion*, New Haven, 1978.

Samuel Kramer, *The Sumerians: Their History, Culture, and Character*, Chicago, 1963.

_____, *History Begins At Sumer: Twenty-seven "Firsts" in Man's Recorded History*, New York, 1959.

_____, *Sumerian Mythology*, rev ed. Philadelphia, 1998.

Miriam Lichtheim, *Ancient Egyptian Literature, Vol. 1, The Old and Middle Kingdoms*, Berkeley, 1975.

_____, *Ancient Egyptian Literature, Vol. 2*, The New Kingdom, Berkeley, 1976.Henrietta McCall, *The Legendary Past: Mesopotamian Myths*, Austin, 1993.

Betty De Shong Meador, *Inanna: Lady of the Largest Heart – Poems of the Sumerian High Priestess, Enheduanna*, Austin, 2000.

James Mellaart, *Catal Huyuk: A Neolithic Town in Anatolia*, New York, 1967.

Marc Van De Mieroop, A History of the Ancient Near East, Cornwall, 2004.

Lewis Mumford, *The City in History*, Boston, 1968.

Hans J. Nissen, *The Early History of the Ancient Near East: 9000 – 2000 B.C.*, Chicago, 1988.

Lorna Oakes and Lucia Gahlin, *Ancient Egypt: An illustrated reference to the myths, religions, pyramids and temples of the land of the pharaohs*, Singapore, 2003.

Steven Olson, *Mapping Human History*, New York, 2003.

Susan Pollock, *Ancient Mesopotamia*, Cambridge, 2010.

James B. Pritchard, ed., *The Ancient Near East: An Anthology of Texts and Pictures*, Princeton, 2011.

Donald B. Redford, *Egypt, Canaan, and Israel in Ancient Times*, Princeton, 1992.

Michael Roaf, *Cultural Atlas of Mesopotamia and the Ancient Near East*, Oxford, 1990.

John Romer, *Testament: The Bible and History*, New York, 1993.

Georges Roux, *Ancient Iraq*, London, 1964.

Chris Scarre, *Smithsonian Timelines of the Ancient World: A Visual Chronology from the Origin of Life to AD 1500*, Washington D. C., 1993.

Tammi J. Schneider, *An Introduction to Ancient Mesopotamian Religion*, Grand Rapids, 2011.

Leonard Shlain, *The Alphabet Versus the Goddess: The Conflict Between Word and Image*, New York, 1998.

Gideon Sjoberg, *The Preindustrial City: Past and Present*, New York, 1960.

Merlin Stone, *When God Was A Woman*, Boston, 1978.

P. J. Vatikiotis, *The History of Modern Egypt*, Baltimore, 1991.

John Walton, *Ancient New Eastern Thought and the Old Testament: Introducing the Conceptual World of the Hebrew Bible*, Grand Rapids, 2006.

Barbara Watterson, *The Egyptians*, Cambridge, 1997.

_____, *Amarna: Ancient Egypt's Age of Revolution*, Brimscombe Port Stroud, 1999.

Diane Wolkstein and Samuel Kramer, *INANNA, Queen of Heaven and Earth: Her Stories and Hymns from Sumer,* New York, 1983.

INDEX

ACKNOWLEDGMENTS

My lovely wife, Loraine, continues to support my book-writing efforts, and for that, I will continue to take out the trash. My son and faithful editor, Malcolm (Randy), was a valuable aide in preparing this book for publication. Janis Monger, a delightful friend, gave particularly useful assistance in the final review of the manuscript.

The support and encouragement of those incredible seniors in UT SAGE is also gratefully acknowledged. Marvin Womack, in particular, kept asking for this book. When I asked Marvin why he had taken my SAGE seminar, Ancient Civilization as Biblical Background, the eight times it was presented, he replied: *"Well, you keep changing it!"* Enjoy, Marvin.